Surviving Brain Damage After Assault

D1630771

At the age of 28, Gary was assaulted by a gang with baseball bats and a hammer, resulting in several skull fractures and severe brain damage. For 19 months, he had little awareness of his surroundings before he started to show some recovery. This inspirational book documents his exceptional journey.

The book presents a series of interviews with Gary, his mother Wendie, who never gave up, the medical team who initially treated him and the therapists who worked with him over a period of 3 years. Through their testimony we learn about the devastating effects which can follow a serious assault to the head and the long process of recovery over several years. With specialist rehabilitation and continuing family support, Gary has exceeded expectations and, apart from some minor physical problems, he is now a normal young man.

Surviving Brain Damage After Assault shows that, contrary to popular belief, considerable gains can be made by people who have experienced a long period of reduced consciousness. The book will be of great value to all professionals working in rehabilitation – psychologists, speech and language therapists, occupational therapists, social workers and rehabilitation doctors, and to people who have sustained a brain injury and their families.

Barbara A. Wilson is a clinical neuropsychologist who has worked in brain injury rehabilitation for nearly 40 years. She has won many awards for her work, including an OBE for services to rehabilitation and three lifetime achievement awards, one from the British Psychological Society, one from the International Neuropsychological Society and one from the National Academy of Neuropsychology. The Division of Neuropsychology has named a prize after her, the Barbara A. Wilson Prize for Distinguished Contributions to Neuropsychology. She is honorary professor

LIVERPOOL JMU LIBRARY

3 1111 01486 3581

at the University of Hong Kong, the University of Sydney and the University of East Anglia.

Samira Kashinath Dhamapurkar is an occupational therapist. Her special interest is in working with people in low awareness states. She worked in India at the Masina Hospital on a psychiatric/drug addiction unit and in a special school for autistic children before coming to the United Kingdom. For the past 5 years, she has worked in the area of neurorehabilitation. In addition to her clinical work, she is also involved in research involving people with disorders of consciousness.

Anita Rose is a consultant neuropsychologist. She works at the Raphael Medical Centre in Tonbridge and also works as an independent consultant neuropsychologist across the globe. She provides significant input in the field of multiple sclerosis via her clinical work, research publications, booklets and consultancy to the MS groups in the UK. She is vice chair for the European Neuropsychology Special Interest Group in MS and acts as a clinical advisor to the MS Society in South Africa.

Surviving Brain Damage After Assault

From Vegetative State to Meaningful Life

Barbara A. Wilson,
Samira Kashinath Dhamapurkar
and Anita Rose

LONDON AND NEW YORK

First published 2016
by Routledge
2 Park Square, Milton Park, Abingdon, Oxfordshire OX14 4RN

and by Routledge
711 Third Avenue, New York, NY 10017

*Routledge is an imprint of the Taylor & Francis Group,
an informa business*

© 2016 Barbara W. Wilson, Samira Kashinath Dhamapurkar
and Anita Rose

The right of Barbara A. Wilson, Samira Dhamapurkar and
Anita Rose to be identified as the authors of this Work has
been asserted by them in accordance with sections 77 and
78 of the Copyright, Designs and Patents Act 1988.

All rights reserved. No part of this book may be reprinted
or reproduced or utilised in any form or by any electronic,
mechanical, or other means, now known or hereafter
invented, including photocopying and recording, or in
any information storage or retrieval system, without
permission in writing from the publishers.

Trademark notice: Product or corporate names may be
trademarks or registered trademarks, and are used only for
identification and explanation without intent to infringe.

British Library Cataloguing in Publication Data
A catalogue record for this book is available from the
British Library

Library of Congress Cataloging-in-Publication Data
Wilson, Barbara A., 1941–
 Surviving brain damage after assault : from vegetative
state to meaningful life / Barbara A. Wilson, Samira
Kashinath Dhamapurkar and Anita Rose.
  pages cm
 Includes bibliographical references and index.
 1. Brain damage—Patients—Rehabilitation. 2. Brain—
Wounds and injuries—Patients—Rehabilitation. 3. Assault
and battery. I. Dhamapurkar, Samira Kashinath. II. Rose,
Anita (Neuropsychologist) III. Title.
 RC387.5.W548 2016
 617.4'81044—dc23
 2015020509

ISBN: 978-1-138-82457-7 (hbk)
ISBN: 978-1-138-82458-4 (pbk)
ISBN: 978-1-315-74060-7 (ebk)

Typeset in Times
by Apex CoVantage, LLC
Printed by Ashford Colour Press Ltd.

MIX
Paper from
responsible sources
FSC
www.fsc.org   FSC® C011748

Contents

Illustrations

Series preface

After Brain Injury: Survivors' Stories was launched in 2014 to meet the need for a series of books aimed at those who have suffered a brain injury and their families and carers. Brain disorders can be life-changing events with far-reaching consequences. However, in the current climate of cuts in funding and service provision for neuropsychological rehabilitation, there is a risk that people whose lives have been transformed by brain injury are left feeling isolated with little support.

So many of the books on brain injury are written for academics and clinicians and filled with technical jargon and are of little help to those directly affected. Instead, this series offers a much-needed personal insight into the experience, as each book is written by a survivor or group of survivors who are living with the very real consequences of brain injury. Each book focuses on a different condition, such as face blindness, amnesia and neglect, or diagnosis, such as encephalitis and locked-in syndrome, resulting from brain injury. Readers will learn about life before the brain injury, the early days of diagnosis, the effects of the brain injury, the process of rehabilitation and life now.

Alongside this personal perspective, professional commentary is also provided by a specialist in neuropsychological rehabilitation. The historical context, neurological state of the art, and data on the condition, including the treatment, outcome and follow-up, will also make these books appealing for professionals working in rehabilitation such as psychologists, speech and language therapists, occupational therapists, social workers and rehabilitation doctors. They will also be of interest to clinical psychology trainees and undergraduate and graduate students in neuropsychology, rehabilitation science and related courses who value the case-study approach as a complement to the more academic books on brain injury.

With this series, we also hope to help expand awareness of brain injury and its consequences. The World Health Organisation has recently acknowledged the need to raise the profile of mental health issues (with the WHO Mental Health Action Plan 2013–20), and we believe there needs to be a similar focus on psychological, neurological and behavioural issues caused by brain disorder and a deeper understanding of the importance of rehabilitation support. Giving a voice to these survivors of brain injury is a step in the right direction.

Barbara A. Wilson

Published titles

Life After Brain Injury
Survivors' Stories
By Barbara A. Wilson, Jill Winegardner, Fiona Ashworth

Identity Unknown
How acute brain disease can destroy knowledge of oneself and others
By Barbara A. Wilson, Claire Robertson, Joe Mole

Surviving Brain Damage After Assault
From Vegetative State to Meaningful Life
By Barbara A. Wilson, Samira Kashinath Dhamapurkar and Anita Rose

Preface

This book tells the story of Gary who, at the age of 28 years, was assaulted by a gang armed with baseball bats and a hammer, resulting in Gary receiving several skull fractures and suffering severe brain damage. He developed hydrocephalus and needed a shunt to drain the fluid from his brain; he also had seizures and later had a piece of bone removed from his skull because his brain was swelling. Eleven months later, surgery was required to replace that bone. Gary had little awareness of his surroundings for nearly 19 months before he started to show some recovery.

How many patients who remain in a state of low awareness for many months go on to regain consciousness? How many of these make a good recovery? There are conflicting answers to these questions ranging from 9% after 6 months to 0% after 12 months (Giacino & Kalmar, 1997) to less than 14% (Multi-Society Task Force Report on PVS, 1994) to 20% (Giacino & Whyte, 2005) and to a high of 33% (Luauté et al., 2010). Most studies seem to agree that the outcome for patients in the vegetative state (VS) is worse than for those in the minimally conscious state (MCS) and that those who are in a state of low awareness following traumatic brain injury do better than those with anoxic or cerebrovascular damage (Giacino & Whyte, 2005). These authors go on to say that "those who recover after one year are typically severely limited in function" (p. 37). Although there are reports of patients recovering consciousness and some functional ability after a long period in a state of disordered consciousness, such patients are relatively few, and they tend to have a shorter period of low awareness. Reimer and LeNavenec (2005) describe a man whose mother was told he was likely to remain vegetative for the rest of his life but is now living in his own home with minimal supervision, walking without assistance, writing legibly, speaking intelligibly and working full time. However, we have no details about the *pattern* or *stages* of his recovery. One reasonably detailed account is provided by Beckinschtein and colleagues (2005), who describe a woman who was in a VS for 2 months and in an MCS for 70 days, a much shorter time than Gary, who is the subject of our book. The woman was followed for 2 years and initially assessed with the Wessex Head Injury Matrix (WHIM; Shiel et al., 2000) – as was Gary. Functional imaging was also carried out, and she had rehabilitation from a multidisciplinary team. She reached an acceptable level of cognitive functioning and regained partial independence. The assessment and treatment offered to this patient was similar to that offered to Gary. This kind of detail is rare, however. There are many patients left in situations in which little or no rehabilitation is offered to them. As Province (2005) points out, these patients cannot speak for themselves and must rely on others to serve as advocates.

The point to make right at the start of our account is that Gary has done exceptionally well, and that after 3 years, he managed to score in the average or above-average range on some neuropsychological tests. At the time of writing (early 2015), he has applied for a college course in electrical engineering, he is playing the guitar, speaks well, makes jokes, can walk in the hydrotherapy pool and, apart from some physical problems, comes across as a normal young man.

Gary was in a rehabilitation centre, where he received several therapies during the many months he spent in a low awareness state. Assessments were carried out continuously, so it has been possible to document his partial recovery over a long period of time. His mother, Wendie, never gives up. She visited Gary almost every day, and he is now at home and receiving ongoing out-patient rehabilitation.

Following some introductory chapters, this book consists of a series of interviews with Gary, his mother, the medical team who initially treated him and the therapists who worked with him over a period of 3 years. Consideration is given as to how much more recovery can be expected and what the future holds for Gary. Through his story, we want to exemplify to rehabilitation staff, medical professionals and families that considerable gains can be made by individuals who have experienced a long period of reduced consciousness. Although Gary will probably not get back to what he was like before the brain injury, he is nevertheless reasonably independent and has a life worth living.

Given the manner in which severe blows to the head are portrayed wrongly in the media as recoverable – sometimes in seconds, minutes or maybe days – it is imperative that the general public is made aware of the devastating effects that can follow a serious assault to the head. The authors of this book aim to make this reality clear to readers and to show the type of care and rehabilitation that people like Gary can receive if we do not give up on them too soon. Unfortunately, many centres would have sent Gary to a nursing home, where he would probably have been left in a low awareness state for the rest of his life. Fortunately, he was referred to the Raphael Medical Centre, where he received excellent care and continuous rehabilitation.

Acknowledgements

We would like first and foremost to thank Gary, Wendie, Zowey and Kelsey for their generous help in providing information to make this book possible. We also thank Mick Wilson and Jessica Fish for reading and commenting on the manuscript and for their very helpful suggestions. A big thank you, too, to Gerhard Florschutz, director of the Raphael Medical Centre, for permission to write about Gary and to all the staff at the Centre engaged in Gary's rehabilitation, particularly Almas Ataie, Imelda Acs, Meiko Aida, David Arikkatt, Lisha Blubert, Costel Bonghene, Melanie Cornell, Costi Cozma, Papiya De, Stanimira Gogova, Shashi Gopaul, Angela Hinchcliffe, Mandy McLeod, Chiara Pavan, Becky Puckett, Tsenka Ruseva, Lorena Salerno, Nick Tomov, Gabor Vajnai and Kenny Urbiztondo. We are grateful to Gareth Davies from the *Croydon Advertiser* for permission to reproduce some of the newspaper reports about Gary. Thanks are also due to John Ling for sending Gary's notes from Kings College Hospital, London, and to Agnes Shiel and Lindsay McLellan for their thoughtful comments on why Gary did so well. We send a special thank you to Matt Wilson for providing the photograph for the front cover. Finally, we wish to thank Lucy Kennedy and Michael Fenton from Psychology Press for their encouragement in writing this book.

Foreword

Barbara Wilson, Samira Kashinath Dhamapurkar and Anita Rose bring us this highly engaging, occasionally gritty and wonderfully uplifting account of Gary, a 28-year-old man who suffered a severe traumatic brain injury following an assault and spent 14 months in a vegetative state and then 5 more months in a minimally conscious state. Through a series of interviews with Gary, his family and the healthcare professionals who cared for him, we witness his remarkable recovery and eventual return to independence. Gary's story is recounted chronologically by family members, others and Gary himself. The events are rolled out in stark detail and are bathed in the thoughts and feelings of those who lived through them. From the harrowing account of the assault that resulted in Gary's brain injury through his carefully planned rehabilitation programme and eventual return home, the reader experiences a birds-eye view of the challenges and triumphs that face those confronted by severe brain injury. As the story unfolds, we learn the facts about brain injury and are then offered a rare view of the deconstruction and resilience of the human spirit.

Over the last decade, the vegetative and minimally conscious states (MCS) have become the focus of intensive scientific study and public interest for a variety of different reasons. A defining feature of MCS is the apparent inconstancy of conscious awareness. In one moment, a person in MCS may exhibit clear-cut behavioural signs of conscious awareness (for example, following simple instructions or signalling "yes" or "no" in response to a question) and then a moment later, for no apparent reason, there is no longer any trace of these behaviours. From a scientific standpoint, therefore, MCS offers an opportunity to better understand the enigma of human consciousness. Persons in

MCS appear to be on the cusp of consciousness, moving back and forth across this critical divide.

Neuroimaging and electroencephalographic (EEG) studies are helping identify structures in the brain that are necessary to support consciousness and the changes that occur during the transition from unconscious to conscious states. From a public policy viewpoint, the MCS syndrome has been controversial since its inception. When the seminal paper on MCS was published in the journal *Neurology* in 2002,[1] it was accompanied by a number of "Letters to the Editor". Some decried the new syndrome as an extension of the "right to die" movement – the idea being that the MCS diagnosis would enable more people to be withdrawn from life support. In reality, this premise was in direct opposition to the authors' original intent to call attention to persons who retain subtle but important signs of conscious awareness. More than a decade later, a great deal of misunderstanding and nihilism around the prospects for recovery persist. In the United States, for example, healthcare insurers often deny requests to authorise rehabilitation services for persons in MCS, arguing that rehabilitation efforts cannot benefit individuals who are unable to actively participate in their care. The bioethicist Joseph J. Fins, MD, has characterised this practice as a civil rights violation occurring within a larger context of "societal neglect".[2]

Gary's story begs the question of whether his remarkable recovery was unusual or even "miraculous". Recent scientific studies investigating long-term outcome following severe TBI suggest that as many as 20% of those who experience prolonged disturbance in consciousness eventually regain functional independence.[3] While the recovery timeline is highly variable, accumulating evidence indicates that meaningful improvements in functional status can occur well after the first year post-injury. These findings challenge existing prognostic wisdom, which holds that recovery can generally be considered complete within 1 year of injury. Unfortunately, we still know very little about which factors predict or interfere with recovery – especially with regard to a single individual. To what extent is recovery influenced by personal history? How important are the unique characteristics of the brain injury? Does the nature and frequency of treatment matter? What role does social support play? These questions remain unanswered. So how do we account for Gary's recovery? For now, readers will have to draw their own conclusions.

Dr Joseph Giacino

Notes

1. Giacino, J.T., Ashwal, S., Childs, N., Cranford, R., Jennett, B., Katz, D.I., Kelly, J.P., Rosenberg, J.H., Whyte, J., Zafonte, R.D., & Zasler, N.D. (2002). The minimally conscious state: Definition and diagnostic criteria. *Neurology, 58*, 349–353.
2. Fins, J.J. (2003). Constructing an ethical stereotaxy for severe brain injury: Balancing risks, benefits and access. *Nature Reviews Neuroscience, 4*, 323–327.
3. Giacino, J., Fins, J., Laureys, S., & Schiff, N. (2014). Disorders of consciousness: The state of the science. *Nature Reviews Neurology, 10*(2), 99–114.

Timeline for Gary

17 December 1982:	Gary born
2 October 2011:	Assault took place. Admitted to King's College Hospital, London
2 & 3 October 2011:	Surgery took place
3 October 2011:	Zowey, Gary's younger sister, starts her diary
8 October 2011:	Gary comes off sedation
13 October 2011:	Gary wakes and starts to talk
1 November 2011:	Gary transferred to Princess Royal Hospital, Bromley (the outskirts of London)
9 November 2011:	Zowey thinks Gary is in the ANGRY stage
10 November 2011:	Zowey stops her diary
25 & 26 November 2011:	Gary has two falls in Princess Royal Hospital
27 November 2011:	Gary is taken back to King's College Hospital
28 November 2011:	Zowey restarts her diary
29 November 2011:	Gary was supposed to go to Blackheath Rehabilitation Centre but instead had the operation to insert the shunt
13 February 2012:	Gary admitted to the Raphael Medical Centre
August 2012:	Cranioplasty performed
April 2013:	Gary emerged from the minimally conscious state
19 June 2014:	Gary received ophthalmic surgery at Maidstone Hospital

August 2014:	Gary moved into a supported-living flat within the RMC and started on a discharge pathway. He started spending longer periods at his mother's house, during which time he attended the RMC daily for outpatient rehabilitation.
November 2014:	Gary makes inquiries about going to college
February 2015:	Gary visited college
March 2015:	Gary is waiting to go for an interview

Chapter 1

Introduction to brain damage part one

When considering traumatic brain injury (TBI), it can be helpful to have knowledge of the basic anatomy of the brain and an awareness of classifications of TBI. This chapter therefore aims to provide the reader with a basic understanding of the brain and its structures and functions. In it, we also discuss ways to classify both TBI severity and prolonged disorders of consciousness, as this will aid the reader in appreciating Gary's remarkable recovery, documented throughout the book.

Basic anatomy of the brain

The brain is a highly complex structure. It contains millions of nerve cells (neurones) and their processes (axons and dendrites), which are established in a highly organised manner. Each individual neurone and its process relies on and is supported by many other cell types, for example, astrocytes (star shaped cells and oligodendrocytes – cells with a few branches).

The brain is divided into several regions that have different functions: the cerebrum is the largest area and is divided into two cerebral hemispheres. The cerebellum is situated beneath the cerebral hemispheres and is connected to the brainstem, which in turn runs into the spinal cord. Each of these areas has a different function, and when damage occurs in an area, changes in the designated function are likely to occur. See Figure 1.1.

Cerebral hemispheres

The left and right cerebral hemispheres control functions for the opposite side of the body. For the majority of people, the left hemisphere is important for verbal skills including language comprehension, speaking and memory for auditory information and written materials. The right hemisphere is

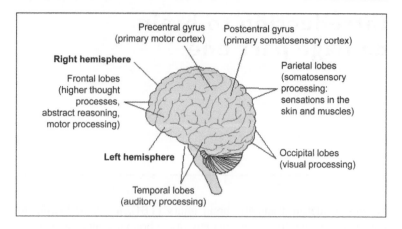

Figure 1.1 The basic anatomy of the brain

Source: Michael W. Eysenck (2013), *Simply Psychology 3rd Edition*, Psychology Press. Reprinted with permission of the Publisher (Taylor and Francis Group, www.informaworld.com).

important for visual skills, including drawing, copying and memory for non-verbal material, such as faces. The two hemispheres are connected by a large bundle of nerve fibres called the corpus callosum, which enables the passing of information from one hemisphere to the other.

Each hemisphere is divided into four lobes. The surface of the brain is folded, with each crest being termed a gyrus and each groove between them a sulcus. The central sulcus separates the frontal from the parietal lobe, and on each side of this sulcus lie the pre-central gyrus (in front) and the post-central gyrus (behind). The pre-central gyrus (motor cortex) is responsible for movement on the opposite side of the body, and the post-central gyrus (sensory cortex) is responsible for appreciation of sensations.

Frontal lobes

These are the front part of the brain and responsible for planning, organisation, problem solving, selective attention, personality, behaviour and emotions. The forward (anterior) part of the frontal lobe, the prefrontal cortex, has an important role in higher cognitive functions and personality. The posterior area of the frontal lobe consists of pre-motor and motor areas. It controls the movement on the opposite side of the body, predominantly via the pre-central gyrus. The lower region of the frontal lobe immediately in front of the pre-central gyrus controls the expression of speech. Damage to both frontal lobes may produce an alteration in personality, a loss of normal inhibitions and incontinence.

The most famous patient with frontal lobe damage is Phineas Gage, a 25-year-old railroad foreman, working in Cavendish, Vermont, in the 19th century. The story is told by Macmillan (2000). In 1848, an incident occurred which was to change our understanding of the relation between mind and brain. Phineas Gage was excavating rock for the railroad company. In preparation for blasting, he was tamping powder into a drill hole. The tamping iron he was holding was over 1 metre long, 6 millimetres in diameter at one end, and weighed 6 kilograms. A premature explosion drove the tamping iron through his left cheek and out of the top of his skull with such force that it threw him on his back. The tamping iron fell several rods behind and was smeared with brain.

Despite his injuries, Gage remained conscious and a few minutes later was sitting in an ox cart writing in his workbook. He recognised and reassured Dr Harlow, who had been summoned to the scene. The wound continued to bleed for two days. A raging infection then followed, rendering Gage semiconscious for a month. His condition was so poor that a coffin had been prepared for him. Nevertheless, Dr Harlow continued treatment, and by the fifth week, the infection had resolved and Gage regained consciousness. He was blind in his left eye and had left facial weakness but presented with no specific deficits to his spine or brain.

Harlow noted that Gage, "Remembers passing and past events correctly, as well before as since the injury. Intellectual manifestations feeble, being exceedingly capricious and childish, but with a will as indomitable as ever; particularly obstinate; will not yield to restraint when it conflicts with his desires." (p. 91). He went on to report that Gage's employers, "who regarded him as the most efficient and capable foreman . . . considered the change in his mind so marked that they could not give him his place again" (p. 92). Harlow felt that although Gage's physical health was good and he was inclined to say that he had recovered,

> "the equilibrium, or balance, so to speak, between his intellectual faculties and his animal propensities seems to have been destroyed. He is fitful, irreverent, indulging at times in the grossest profanity (which was not previously his custom), manifesting but little deference for his fellows, impatient of restraint or advice when it conflicts

with his desires, at times pertinaciously obstinate, yet capricious and vacillating, devising many plans of future operation, which are no sooner arranged than they are abandoned. . . . in this regard his mind was radically changed, so decidedly that his friends said that he was 'no longer Gage'" (Macmillan, 2000, pp. 92–93).

Another possible victim of frontal lobe damage was King Henry VIII of England (Worsely, 2009). Henry's first serious accident occurred in 1524, in a jousting accident, when he failed to lower the visor on his helmet and was hit by his opponent's lance just above the right eye, after which he frequently suffered from migraines. On 24 of January 1536, 44-year-old Henry, in full armour, was thrown from his horse, itself armoured, which then fell on top of him. He was unconscious for 2 hours and was thought at first to have been fatally injured. Since that time, it has been noted by a number of historical observers that Henry appeared to be less generous, more paranoid and quite frightening to his immediate subjects and associates, most of whom had to tread on eggshells in his presence. Although, in this case, the possible effects of brain damage can only be surmised, the evidence of a radical change in the king's behaviour is not insubstantial. It has to be said that very few historians, with the exception of Worsely, have commented on the possibility of brain damage suffered by King Henry, but maybe this has more to do with their own limited knowledge of the possible effects of 2 hours of unconsciousness rather than their more profound knowledge of King Henry's interactions with courtiers and politicians who would have found it impossible to pierce the bubble of court etiquette in the presence of their 'divine' but intolerant leader? Maybe his many future wives could have commented had they been allowed?

Parietal lobes

These lobes control the appreciation of sensation largely via the post-central gyrus. They contain the primary sensory cortex which controls the experience of sensation – touch and pressure. The lower region of the parietal lobe plays an important role in the understanding of speech and language and performing calculations. Nerve fibres from the optic nerves (controlling vision) pass deeply through the parietal lobes to eventually reach the occipital lobes.

Damage to the right parietal lobe can cause visual spatial defects, and damage to the left parietal lobe can disturb a person's written and spoken language capabilities.

For an interesting account of a soldier who sustained left parietal lobe damage, see Luria's classic book, *The Man With The Shattered World: History of a Brain Wound* (Luria, 1987; translated by Luria & Solotaroff, 1987). The book is written partly by the survivor, called "Z", and partly by the neuropsychologist, Alexandr Romanov Luria, who is often called "the grandfather of neuropsychology". Z received a gunshot wound to the head during the Second World War. He first met Luria 3 months later. His major injury was to the parieto-occipital region of the left hemisphere. Because his frontal lobes were undamaged, Z was able to recognise his difficulties and tried to overcome them. The book describes how he spent 25 years attempting to conquer his many severe problems, including memory, language, reading, writing and spatial difficulties.

Occipital lobes

The occipital lobes are the regions at the back of the brain and are involved in processing visual information. Although they are the receptive areas for visual information, they also play an important role in visual recognition of shapes and colours. Damage to one occipital lobe would produce a deficit in vision that would affect the visual field in both eyes, making it difficult to see peripheral objects in one direction only. It would not cause blindness – this would only be caused by severe damage to both occipital lobes.

One man with a posterior cerebral artery stroke affecting the occipital and temporal areas bilaterally is H.J.A. (John), who worked with Glyn Humphreys and Jane Riddoch, two well-known British researchers specialising in perceptual problems. John was left with visual object agnosia (an inability to recognise objects despite adequate eyesight and naming ability) together with other vision-dependent problems, including face recognition, word recognition, reading and finding his way around the environment. Two books have been written about John (Humphreys & Riddoch, 1987, 2013), providing important insights into our understanding of object recognition processes.

Temporal lobes

The temporal lobes play an important role in memory, with the right side mainly involved in visual memory and the left in verbal memory. It would often require damage to both temporal lobes to cause a severe memory disturbance. The upper portion of the temporal lobe on the dominant area for language, (usually the left side), also plays an important role in the understanding of speech and language, along with the adjacent parietal lobe. Nerve fibres from the optic nerves (controlling vision) also pass deeply through the temporal lobes to eventually reach the occipital lobes.

A fascinating and moving account of a man with severe temporal lobe damage and dense amnesia following herpes simplex viral encephalitis (HSVE) is written by his wife, Deborah Wearing (2005), who tells the story of her husband, Clive, one of the best-known amnesic patients in the United Kingdom (Wearing, 2005; Wilson, 1999; Wilson, Baddeley, & Kapur, 1995; Wilson, Kopelman, & Kapur, 2008). Clive, a professional musician, conductor and world expert on the Renaissance composer Orlando Lassus, became ill with HSVE in March 1985. He has one of the most severe cases of amnesia on record: he cannot retain information for more than a few seconds, he cannot learn new information and he has lost much of the knowledge about his earlier life. There are several video clips about Clive on YouTube.

A different kind of problem following temporal lobe damage was sustained by Claire, who, like Clive, was a survivor of HSVE. She was left with very severe prosopagnosia (an inability to recognise faces) together with a loss of knowledge of people's identities (Wilson, Robertson, & Mole, 2015). In the book *Identity Unknown*, we learn of Claire's journey as told in her words, the words of her family and the rehabilitation therapists who worked alongside her. "Her poignant and honest recollections highlight the need for psychologists, clinicians, doctors and therapists to listen to and hear the voices of the patients that they assess and treat if we are to have a greater empathy with our clients and develop appropriate rehabilitation supports" (Dewar, 2014 p. xiv).

Cerebellum

The cerebellum controls coordination in the limbs and the trunk by receiving information from sense organs via the spinal cord and input from the cerebral hemispheres. Damage here may impair coordination of limb movements and cause unsteadiness of gait.

Jenny, who sustained cerebellar and occipital lobe damage, following a horse riding accident, was left with unsteadiness of gait and cerebellar dysarthria (poor articulation and shaky speech caused by damage to the muscles controlling the speech mechanisms). An account of Jenny and her rehabilitation can be found in Wilson (1999).

Brainstem

All nerve fibres connecting the cerebral hemispheres with the cerebellum and spinal cord pass through the brainstem, controlling all functions in the limbs and body. There are also collections of neurones (nuclei) in the brainstem that control many functions in the head and neck, particularly eye movements, facial sensation and movement, swallowing and coughing. Areas within the brainstem also control consciousness, breathing, heart rate and blood pressure, and as these vital nerves all lie very close together in the brainstem, even a small area of damage might produce multiple severe deficits.

Brainstem damage can result in locked-in syndrome (LIS), a rare consequence of brain damage. Patients with LIS are fully conscious but unable to move or speak due to paralysis of nearly all voluntary muscles except the eyes. The best known case is probably that of Jean-Dominique Bauby, who "wrote" *The Diving Bell and the Butterfly* (1997) by means of a painstaking dictation system involving Bauby blinking when the letter he wanted to use was read aloud from a letter series organised by frequency. The condition is typically caused by a lesion in the pontine area, usually a stroke in the basilar artery or a pontine haemorrhage. A more recent personal account is that of Tracey, who sustained LIS following an accident at the gym (Wilson & Okines, 2014). Another survivor of brainstem damage who was not locked in but had severe physical and articulation problems is Kate, whose story is told in Wilson and Bainbridge (2014).

Chapter 2

Introduction to brain damage part two

Other important structures of the brain

The limbic system (see Figure 2.1)

This area of the brain was once known as the "fifth lobe" of the brain. It contains the olfactory pathways, the amygdala and the hippocampus. The hypothalamus is also situated within this area. It is involved in integration of recent memory, biological rhythms, sexual drive, fear, anger and emotions. Damage to this area can result in loss of the sense of smell, libido issues, agitation, loss of emotional control and deficits in recent memory. People with Alzheimer's disease, severe amnesia and Kluver-Bucy syndrome (visual recognition problems, loss of normal fear and anger responses and sometimes hypersexuality; Lippe, Gonin-Flambois, & Jambaqué, 2012) are likely to have damage to limbic system structures. The patient described in Wilson (1982) was originally described as having Kluver-Bucy syndrome. Following a cerebral vascular accident, he presented with hypersexuality, visual recognition problems and severe amnesia. When he was seen for rehabilitation, the recognition problems and hypersexuality had reduced, while the severe amnesia remained.

Basal ganglia

This is the processing link between the thalamus and the motor cortex. It has responsibility for initiation and direction of voluntary movement, inhibitory balance and postural reflexes. Damage in this area can result in movement disorders, tremors, difficulty in initiation of movements and increase in muscle tone. Damage in this area can result in a whole host of difficulties, including Huntington's disease and Parkinson's disease. For

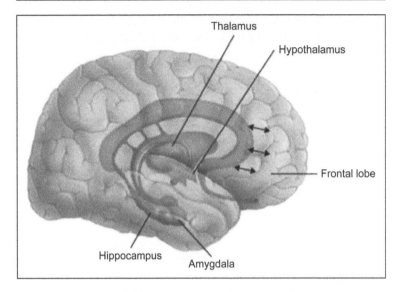

Figure 2.1 The limbic system

Source: Wilson and Wilson (2015), *Understanding Emotional Development*, Psychology Press. Reprinted with permission of the Publisher (Taylor and Francis Group, www.informaworld.com).

one family's account of living with Huntington's disease, see Sulaiman (2007), and for personal accounts of Parkinson's disease see Ashford and colleagues (2013).

Thalamus

This is the processing centre of the cerebral cortex and co-ordinates and regulates all functional activity of the cortex via the integration of the input of information to the brain. It does not, however, process olfactory input. The thalamus also contributes to emotional expression. Damage to this area can produce altered states of consciousness, loss of perception and a condition called thalamic syndrome, also known as Dejerine–Roussy syndrome, in which the individual can experience spontaneous pain on the opposite side of the body from the location of the brain damage. No personal accounts of people suffering from this could be found, although damage to the thalamus is frequently seen after stroke and encephalitis. Kate, mentioned earlier, had damage to both thalami (Menon et al., 1998). Kate had no major cognitive deficits, but some people may have memory, attention and executive problems (Van der Werf et al., 2003). A recent book about the thalamus is by Douglas (2014).

Hypothalamus

This area is responsible for hormone production, which governs body temperature, thirst, hunger, sleep, circadian rhythm, moods and sex drive. It is known as the integration centre of the autonomic nervous system and is involved in the regulation of body temperature and the endocrine system. It also plays a role in physical expression of behaviour, appetite control and pleasure. The anterior hypothalamus is involved with para-sympathetic activity: in other words, it plays a "maintenance" role. The posterior hypothalamus is involved with sympathetic activity such as the "flight or fight" response and also takes a role in stress regulation. Damage to this area causes hormonal imbalance, inability to control temperature, inappropriate antidiuretic hormone release, diabetes insipidus and failure to thrive. Jenny (Wilson, 1999) had problems with temperature control and always felt hot. Even in very cold weather, she could not bear to wear long sleeves or a coat. Another patient known to us wore a special device which measured his temperature and beeped if he became too hot or too cold in order to alert him to regulate his temperature through other means.

Brain injury

Definition of acquired brain injury

Acquired brain injury (ABI) is defined as non-degenerative injury to the brain occurring since birth. It includes traumatic brain injuries (TBI's), strokes, brain illness such as encephalitis and any other kind of brain injury acquired after birth.

Definition of a traumatic brain injury

Traumatic brain injury (TBI) is defined as an alteration in brain function or other evidence of brain pathology caused by an external force (Menon et al., 2010). It is not an injury that is degenerative or congenital in nature but is caused by external physical force that may produce a diminished or altered state of consciousness, which results in an impairment of cognitive abilities or physical functioning.

There are many systems used to classify TBI, including severity, type (for example, diffuse axonal injury or haemorrhages), and outcome and prognosis.

There are three generally acknowledged levels of severity of TBI which are based on the Mayo Classification System for Traumatic Brain Injury Severity (2007). This system was recently compared against single indicators such as post-traumatic amnesia (PTA), Glasgow Coma Scale (GCS) and loss of consciousness in order to ascertain the usefulness of such a multiple-indicator system (Friedland & Hutchinson, 2013). The comparison highlighted that the Mayo system far outperformed any single indicator in classifying severity of TBI, with outcome results of sensitivity and specificity for moderate and severe being 89% and 98%, respectively.

The three levels of severity are:

Mild traumatic brain injury, which is a trauma to the head that results in a confused state or a loss of consciousness of less than 30 minutes, the initial Glasgow Coma Scale of 13 to 15, and post-traumatic amnesia lasts less than 24 hours.

Moderate traumatic brain injury, which is a trauma to the head that results in a loss of consciousness of 30 minutes to 24 hours, an initial Glasgow Coma Scale of 9 to 12. Post-traumatic amnesia can last 24 hours to 7 days.

Severe traumatic brain injury, which is a trauma to the head that results in a loss of consciousness of greater than 24 hours, an initial Glasgow Coma Scale of 3 to 8, and a post-traumatic amnesia period of greater than seven days.

Classification of prolonged disorders of consciousness

Following severe brain injury, many patients progress through stages of coma, vegetative state (VS) and minimally conscious state (MCS) as they emerge into a state of full awareness. For those who do not emerge into the state of full awareness, the umbrella classification is that of being in a prolonged disorder of consciousness (PDOC). In the words of the late Bryan Jennett, "The strange and harrowing sight of a person who is awake but unaware, with no evidence of a working mind, provokes intense debate among scientists, health professionals, philosophers ethicists and lawyers" (Jennett, 2005, p. 163). Jennett (ibid.) and Kalmar and Giacino (2005) say that legally, the VS can be declared permanent after 12 months for those who have sustained a TBI and after 6 months for those who are in the VS from non-traumatic causes. The Royal College of Physicians in London produced guidelines saying that long-term or prolonged disorders of consciousness (DOC) is defined as any DOC persisting for four or more weeks (Royal College of Physicans (RCP) Guidelines, 2013).

In order to diagnose a patient with PDOC, there has to be an understanding of what we mean by consciousness. The definition of the term "consciousness" considers two parameters, wakefulness and awareness. In defining "wakefulness", it is recognised this is a state in which the eyes are open and there is a degree of motor arousal. This is in contrast to sleep, which is a state of eye closure and motor inertness. "Awareness", however is the ability to have and the having of experience of any kind.

While this definition is helpful in understanding the construct of consciousness in terms of assessing an individual's level of awareness, there is no simple, single clinical sign or test that can be used to ascertain whether indeed an individual is aware. The presence of awareness can only be inferred from a range of behaviours which indicate that an individual can recognise self and the world around them and can indicate intentional behaviours and interact with others.

In terms of diagnosis, the following criteria are well recognised (Giacino & Kalmar, 2005; Giacino et al., 2002; RCP, 2013):

Coma: This is a state of absent wakefulness and absent awareness. The individual is in a state of un-arousable unresponsiveness lasting more than 6 hours. In this state, the person:

- cannot be awakened,
- fails to respond normally to painful stimuli, light or sound,
- lacks a normal sleep–wake cycle, *and*
- does not initiate voluntary actions.

Vegetative state (VS): This is a state of wakefulness without awareness in which there are sleep–wake cycles and noted reflexive and spontaneous behaviours. However, there is a complete absence of behavioural evidence of self- or environmental awareness. This state was originally described by Kretschmer (1940), who called it the "Apallic Syndrome" from the Greek meaning "without cortex". Jennett and Plum (1972) introduced the term "vegetative state" (meaning like a plant) to describe behaviour, but VS can be seen as a dehumanising label implying hopelessness (Province, 2005); it is no wonder that many relatives understand it to mean "vegetable". Laureys and colleagues (2010) suggested the term "unresponsive wakefulness syndrome" but, to date, this has not been widely accepted.

Minimally conscious state (MCS): This is a state of severely altered consciousness in which there is minimal but clearly discernible behavioural evidence of self- or environmental awareness. A person who is in MCS will show evidence of inconsistent but reproducible responses that cannot be categorised as reflexive or spontaneous. They will also indicate some level of interaction with the environment around them.

As highlighted by the Working Party of the Royal College of Physicians in their report (2013), the hallmark of a minimally conscious state "is that the interactions and behavioural responses are inconsistent, but reproducible".

Despite these criteria suggesting that there are clear-cut differences between VS and MCS, in practice, it can be very difficult to divide these boundaries. In the 1990s, the rate of misdiagnosis of VS was between 37% and 43% (Andrews, 1997; Childs, Mercer, & Childs, 1993). More than a decade later, Schnakers and Laureys (2014) found that, of 44 people diagnosed with a VS, 41% were misdiagnosed (almost no better than flipping a coin). Beckinschtein and colleagues (2005) suggest that we should view VS and MCS as a continuum rather than as separate categories.

Emergence from MCS: This is indicated by the recovery of reliable and consistent responses. In attempting to define this, the U.S. Aspen Work Group (Giacino et al., 2002) proposed that emergence from MCS is characterised by the evidence of reliable and consistent demonstration of one or both of the following:

1. Functional interactive communication
2. Functional use of objects

However, it has to be noted that the upper levels of MCS versus emergence from MCS can be difficult to define. In order to support the diagnosis of such a recovery, the Working Party of the Royal College of Physicians in their report (2013) proposed a brief set of operational parameters which expanded that of the Aspen group. The recommendation is that emergence from MCS is characterised by the evidence of reliable and consistent demonstration in at least one of the following:

1. Functional use of objects
2. Consistent discriminatory choice making
3. Functional interactive communication
4. Evidence of awareness of self
5. Evidence of awareness of environment

They also recommended the use of standardised biographical and situational questions together with these parameters.

When considering PDOC, it is important to note they are distinct from the conditions of locked-in syndrome and brainstem death.

Locked-in syndrome (LIS): This condition usually is the result of brainstem pathology, which disrupts the voluntary control of movement. However, the sustained damage does not disturb wakefulness or awareness. Individuals who are diagnosed as "locked in" usually experience significant if not full body paralysis, but they are fully conscious. Such individuals are able to communicate consistently and reliably using movements of the eyes or by movements of the eyelids. The American Congress of Rehabilitation Medicine (1995) said that the LIS had five characteristics, namely (i) sustained eye opening, (ii) preserved basic cognitive abilities, (iii) aphonia or severe hypophonia (loss of voice), (iv) quadriplegia or quadriparesis and (v) a vertical or lateral eye movement or blinking of the upper eyelid as the primary means of communication. In order to determine whether someone has LIS, one can ask a series of yes/no questions, ask the person to blink once for yes and twice for no (or eyes up for yes and down for no) and see if the responses are accurate. Laureys and colleagues (2005) published an excellent chapter on what it is like to have this syndrome.

Brainstem death: This clinical syndrome is defined by the absence of all brainstem functions. This is confirmed by the absence of brainstem reflexes throughout the pathway of the brainstem. The individual will have permanently lost the capacity for consciousness and the ability to breathe.

Recovering from traumatic brain injury

Although a good understanding of how people recover from TBI would help us plan and monitor our rehabilitation services, enable us to give better advice to families and allow us to improve the focus of rehabilitation, it is true to say that such understanding remains limited in society.

Wilson (2010) has written about recovery, and her paper is summarised and updated here. "Recovery" means to return to a normal state of health, but most people with severe brain injury will rarely if ever regain all the functions, abilities and skills they had prior to the brain injury. Jennett and Bond's (1975) alternative interpretation of recovery as the resumption of normal life even though there may be minor neurological or psychological deficits is possible for some survivors of TBI. Recovery has also been defined as the diminution of impairments in behavioural or physiological functions over time (Marshall, 1985), and this is likely to occur for the majority of patients. Perhaps the definition of recovery that most closely reflects the situation for the majority of people with brain damage is that described by Bryan Kolb (1995), himself a survivor of stroke, when he suggested that recovery typically involves *partial* return of function together with substitution of function. From our observations, this is probably the definition of recovery that most closely reflects the situation for the majority of people with brain damage.

Natural recovery from brain damage

It is now generally accepted that acquired brain injuries, such as stroke or trauma, initiate a cascade of regenerative events that last for at least several weeks, if not months (Nudo, 2013). Brain damage resulting from TBI can be caused by both primary and secondary causes. Primary damage occurs as a direct result of the accident or insult, such as contusions (bruising of brain tissue) or shearing of axons, while secondary damage is caused by complications arising from the initial injury, such as reduced blood pressure or infections. If secondary damage is avoided through expert medical care, then the final outcome or recovery is maximised. Miller, Pentland and Berrol (1990) suggested that the final outcome of any patient who suffers head injury is governed by three groups of factors: the pre-injury status of the brain, the total amount of damage done to the brain by the impact of the head injury (primary damage) and the cumulative effect of the secondary damage – pathological damage to the already injured brain. Secondary damage may result in more permanent disability than primary damage even though it is potentially avoidable (Daisley et al., 2009).

Although recovery from TBI is variable, far from uniform and may, in some individuals, continue for years (Millis et al., 2001), most survivors undergo some and often considerable recovery. This is likely to be fairly rapid in the early weeks and months post-injury, followed by a slower recovery that can continue for many years. A similar pattern may be seen following other kinds of non-progressive injury including stroke, encephalitis and hypoxia. In these latter cases, however, the recovery process may last months rather than years. A recent paper by Rosenblum (2015), particularly concerned with patients in long-lasting coma, suggests that recovery is possible if critical connections between the brainstem inputs and the ascending arousal system are spared.

Factors influencing recovery from brain damage

A number of factors influence the extent of recovery, some of which we can do nothing about once the damage has occurred. These include the age of the person at the time of insult, severity of damage, location of damage, the status of undamaged areas of the brain and the premorbid cognitive status of the brain. Other factors such as motivation, family support systems and the quality of rehabilitation available can be manipulated

Age, gender and cognitive reserve are three major factors that could affect recovery after TBI. In 1940, Kennard showed that young primates with lesions in the motor and premotor cortexes exhibited sparing and partial recovery of motor function. Her findings came to be known as "the Kennard principle", and it is this which may account for the belief that children recover better than adults from an insult to the brain (Johnson, Rose, Brooks, & Eyers, 2003). Even Kennard, however, recognised that such sparing did not always occur and that some problems became worse over time. Some studies have shown that younger children, particularly those below the age of 2 years, fare worse in the long term than do older children (Anderson et al., 2006; Forsyth et al., 2001; Hessen, Nestvold, & Anderson, 2007; Konczak et al., 2005). Studies suggesting the opposite (Montour-Proulx et al., 2004) or no difference (Mosch et al., 2005) are looking at children with focal rather than diffuse lesions. Tavano and colleagues (2014), among others, found no neuroprotective effect of age. Older people, however, may do less well, and a recent paper suggests that those aged 65 years or more have an increased risk of developing dementia (Johnson & Stewart, 2014).

As well as age, there are other, perhaps more important factors that have to be considered as contributing to the recovery process, such as whether the lesion is focal or diffuse (Levin, 2003); the actual severity of the insult; and the time since acquisition of the function under consideration. For example, someone who has just learned to read at the time of the insult is more likely to show reading deficits than is someone who learned to read many years before.

In 1987, Attella, Nattinville and Stein suggested that female animals may be protected against the effects of brain injury at certain stages of their cycle due to the effects of oestrogen and progesterone. This was confirmed by Roof and Hall (2000). Potentially important for rehabilitation (Stein, 2007), progesterone has been given to survivors of TBI, with some indication that this leads to a better outcome (Wright et al., 2007). Additionally, some studies have considered the long-term outcome for females and males following TBI. The findings are contradictory: for example, Ratcliff and colleagues (2007) suggested that females do better than males, while other studies indicate the opposite (Farace & Alves, 2000; Ponsford et al., 2008). The Ponsford and associates study controlled for Glasgow Coma Scale score, age and cause of injury and found that females had both a lower rate of survival and a lower rate of good outcome at 6 months post-injury. The authors thought this might be due to the fact that more females died in the early stages. In general, they found no evidence that women did better and some evidence that they did worse than males. The debate continues, with Skolnick and colleagues (2014) suggesting no differences between males and females in a large randomised control trial, while Cancelliere, Donovan and Cassidy (2015) found small sex differences for some outcomes for mild TBI.

People whose brain injuries are in similar locations and of the same severity and extent may, nevertheless, have very different problems and outcomes. Recognition of this has led to the development of the concept of cognitive reserve, which is the third factor to be considered in the understanding of recovery from brain injury. The principle of cognitive reserve suggests that people with more education and high intelligence may show less impairment than those with poor education and low intelligence. This might be because individuals with high intelligence may process tasks in a more efficient way (Stern, 2007). As a consequence, in some cases of Alzheimer's disease, task impairment manifests itself later in the disease because of such cognitive reserve. Most clinicians are aware of the fact that any insult of the same severity can produce profound damage in one patient and minimal damage in another. This may also explain differences in recovery following non-progressive brain injury: as Symonds has argued in an often-quoted remark, "It is not only the kind of head injury that matters but the kind of head" (1937, p. 109).

There are two separate models of cognitive reserve, one being a passive model, which depends on the number of neurons possessed by an individual or the person's brain size, and the other an active model in which the brain uses its cognitive processing strategies or compensatory techniques to deal with any damage.

Bigler (2007) believes that the passive model of cognitive reserve helps explain not only initial recovery from TBI but also recovery across a lifespan; and it allows us to understand why there is an increased risk of dementia in survivors of TBI. Schutz (2007) focuses on the active model of cognitive reserve in a report on nine highly successful survivors of severe TBI who were far more successful than their peers in cognitive, academic and social achievements because they implemented

LIVERPOOL JOHN MOORES UNIVERSITY
LEARNING SERVICES

procedures to minimise the impact of their deficits. This concept is further supported by Schneider and colleagues (2014). This American study recruited 769 survivors of a TBI who were at least 23 years old. One year later, only 10% of those with low education had no disability and had returned to work, compared to 28% of those who had gone to college and 39% of those with a college degree. The authors concluded that people with a college degree were seven times more likely to make a good recovery from their injury than were those who did not complete high school. A recent review of cognitive reserve can be found in Nunnari, Bramanti and Marino (2014).

How does recovery occur?

Although our knowledge of the process of recovery remains limited, it is likely that it involves different biological processes, including plasticity of the central nervous system (CNS), such as the reorganisation of the pre-existing network and axonal sprouting (Taupin, 2006). For example, changes seen in the first few minutes after a mild head injury, with no permanent structural damage, are probably due to the resolution of temporary dysfunction, indicating that structures are nonfunctioning because of shock but are not destroyed. Robertson and Murre (1999) refer to something similar when they say that plastic re-organisation may occur because of a rapidly occurring alteration in synaptic activity taking place over seconds or minutes. Recovery after several days is more likely to be due to resolution of temporary structural abnormalities such as oedema (swelling) or vascular disruption (damage to the blood vessels; Jennett, 1990) or to the depression of metabolic enzyme activity (changes in chemical reactions; Whyte, 1990). Recovery after months or years is even less well understood. Regeneration, diaschisis and plasticity are three possible ways this can occur (Stein & Hoffman, 2003).

Regeneration refers to the re-growth of neurons following brain damage. For regeneration to take place, it is necessary for new cells and axons to survive and integrate into existing neural networks (Johansson, 2007). Logan, Oliver and Berry (2007) believe that neurons do begin to re-grow initially, but this ceases as scarring of fibres occurs, preventing reconnection of severed neuronal pathways. Consequently, functional recovery from such injuries is poor. Voss and colleagues (2006), however, argue that axonal re-growth may take place many years after severe brain injury, and they report on one patient who regained functional speech despite being in a minimally conscious state for 19 years.

Several studies have suggested that cell implantation can also lead to regeneration. Ma, et al. (2007) found that bone marrow stromal cells can promote recovery from TBI when injected directly into the brain or the cerebrospinal fluid or the bloodstream. The authors caution that there are many problems to be solved – as recognised by Parr, Tator and Keating (2007), who point out that the transplantation of bone marrow cells is unlikely to be a major factor in recovery from TBI. They think that other factors such as neuro-protection and enriched environments play a greater role. Taupin (2006) claims that after TBI and stroke, new neuronal cells are generated at the sites of injury, where they replace some of the degenerated nerve cells, showing that the CNS is attempting to regenerate itself. One of the latest studies investigating cell implantation is that of Sharma and associates (2015), who said that cell therapy may promote functional recovery, leading to an improved quality of life in chronic TBI.

The widely held belief for many years was that cerebral plasticity is severely restricted in the adult human brain. This is no longer tenable, as there is now sufficient evidence to show that some regeneration of brain cells does occur after brain damage. Taupin (2006) argues that there is a great deal of neurological recovery in the months and years following brain damage despite frequently occurring permanent structural damage. What is less clear, however, is the extent to which regeneration can lead to useful gains in coping with real-life problems. Nudo (2013) believes that behavioural experience is one of the most potent ways to change cortical functions.

Diaschisis is a term first used by Von Monakow in 1914 (Finger et al., 2004). It assumes that damage to a specific area of the brain can result in neural shock or disruption elsewhere in the brain. This could be adjacent to the site of the primary insult or much farther away (Miller, 1984). In either case, the shock follows a particular neural route. Robertson and Murre (1999, p. 547) interpret diaschisis as "a weakening of synaptic connections between the damaged and undamaged sites". Because cells in the two areas are no longer firing together, synaptic connectivity between them is weakened, resulting in the lowering of functioning in the undamaged but partly disconnected remote site.

Plasticity is the third mechanism by which recovery can take place. Although in the neuroscience literature the term "plasticity" refers to both positive and negative responses to environmental factors and to insults to the brain, amongst brain injury rehabilitation specialists, the term refers to anatomical re-organisation whereby an undamaged part of the brain can take over the functioning of a damaged area. In Duffau's

(2006) words, cerebral plasticity is "the dynamic potential of the brain to reorganise itself during ontogeny, learning, or following damage" (Duffau, 2006, p. 885). Until a few years ago, this idea was discredited as an explanation for recovery in adults, although recently views have begun to change. Bütefisch (2004) argues that the human adult brain retains the ability to reorganise itself throughout life. Cecatto and Chadi (2007) suggest that behavioural experience and neuronal stimulation play a part in modifying the functional organisation of remaining cortical tissue and can lead to clinical improvements.

Robertson (2002) argues that recovery is rapid for deficits that are subserved by multiple circuits such as unilateral neglect and slowest for deficits that are subserved by a more limited number of circuits such as hemianopia, the reason being that in the latter there are fewer alternative pathways available to take over the functioning of the damaged pathways. This could be the reason language functions appear to show better recovery over time than do memory functions (Kolb, 1995).

Robertson and Murre (1999) believe there are two mechanisms which can cause plastic re-organisation. The first is due to a rapidly occurring alteration in synaptic activity taking place over seconds or minutes, while the second is because of structural changes taking place over days and weeks. The authors posit that some people show spontaneous recovery with no specific intervention; others show very little recovery, even over a period of years – and compensatory approaches should be used with these people. Still others show reasonably good recovery provided they receive rehabilitation, and these are described as the assisted recovery group, with whom one can address issues of plasticity. Robertson and Murre also believe that the severity of brain damage determines grouping: Mild lesions result in spontaneous recovery; people with moderate lesions benefit from assisted recovery; and those with severe lesions require the compensatory approach.

Although there may be some truth in this, the idea may be too neatly or tightly packaged. For example, the location of the lesion almost certainly plays a role in rehabilitation: people with mild lesions in the frontal lobes, for instance, could be more disadvantaged in terms of recovery than people with severe lesions in the left anterior temporal lobe. The former group might have attention, planning and organisation problems precluding them from gaining the maximum benefit from the rehabilitation on offer, whereas the latter group, with language problems, could show considerable plasticity by transferring some of the language functions to the right hemisphere. All those who do not show spontaneous recovery, however, require rehabilitation, which could focus on attempts to restore lost functioning or help people compensate for their everyday problems or, as is often the case in rehabilitation, require a combination of the two. What kind of rehabilitation is available and what evidence is there that it is effective?

There are a few accounts of recovery from the VS and the MCS (see, for example, Reimer & LeNavenec, 2005, and Beckinschtein et al., 2005). Wilson, Gracey and Bainbridge (2001) also describe the cognitive recovery of a young woman who survived ADEM (acute disseminated encephalomyelitis). Dewar, Pickard and Wilson (2008) followed up five patients in the vegetative state and seven in the minimally conscious state at least 2 years after initial contact to investigate whether there had been any improvement. Initially, all had been assessed on the Wessex Head Injury Matrix, so at follow-up, this was re-administered. In addition, the Functional Independence Measure, the Rivermead Motor Index and a psychosocial questionnaire were administered to explore functional and psychosocial outcome. Most of the patients showed some improvement, but all were still very dependent physically, and all required a high level of support in their activities of daily living.

Chapter 3

Imaging procedures in understanding brain injury

Most patients admitted to hospital with a brain injury or infection will have a computed tomography (CT) brain scan. CT scans use computer-processed X-rays to produce pictures of slices of the brain to enable us to see the structure of the brain without the need for surgery. Thus, these scans provide a rough-and-ready picture of any damage that has occurred. They are limited, however, as some parts of the brain may be partly obscured and certain types of damage may be undetected. A more sophisticated scan is a magnetic resonance imaging (MRI) scan. These are increasingly used with TBI patients. This type of imaging procedure employs strong magnetic fields and radio waves to form images. Although an MRI scan is better than a CT scan at detecting the extent and severity of a brain injury (Coleman et al., 2007), it is not always readily available, and CT scans are more likely to be used immediately after a TBI. Another kind of MRI is diffusion tensor imaging (DTI). This allows one to visualise anatomical connections in the brain and can detect changes in white matter. Consequently, it has become popular in helping in the understanding of neurological disorders including TBI. Voelbel, Genova, Chiaravalotti and Hoptman (2012) believe this may be a good measure to detect neuroplasticity in patients undergoing cognitive rehabilitation. Their paper, however, does not address people with disorders of consciousness (DOC).

Both CT and MRI scans produce structural images or images of a still brain. Even more sophisticated imaging involves functional imaging in which the brain can be seen in action. These include functional MRI (fMRI), positron emission tomography (PET) and single photon emission tomography (SPECT). When an area of the brain is in use because it is engaged in a particular activity such as speaking or thinking or imagining something, blood flow to that area increases. This is what is measured in an fMRI scan. Because fMRI does not require injections, surgery, the taking of substances or exposure to radiation, it is popular in research studies. For a PET scan, a radioactive tracer is introduced into the body, allowing the scanner to detect rays that are emitted and, from these, it can produce a three-dimensional image. A PET scan can identify many complex aspects of the brain but it is mainly a research tool that is expensive and not widely available (Coleman et al. (2007)). Because PET scans expose people to radiation, they cannot be used as frequently as fMRI, and women of child bearing age are not allowed to be used as research subjects. SPECT scans use radiation to measure cerebral blood flow. Although it is a relatively simple and inexpensive technique, it tends to produce rather poor images.

All types of scans, including SPECT, PET and fMRI scans, have been used in research with people with disorders of consciousness to see if there is residual cognitive functioning in such patients. One of the very first, if not the first PET study to assess a patient in the VS, was the study by Menon and colleagues (1998). The authors used PET to study the covert cognitive processing of a 26-year-old woman with acute, disseminated encephalomyelitis described as being in a "persistent vegetative state". She showed evidence of perceiving visual stimuli and of processing these, as her responses to photographs of familiar faces differed from responses to scrambled images with the same colours and brightness. This woman went on to regain consciousness, and when neuropsychologically assessed, she was shown to have good cognitive functioning (Wilson, Gracey, & Bainbridge, 2001).

Other interesting studies include those reported by Boly and associates (2005). They used PET and fMRI to look at patients in the VS and the MCS and report that "Despite an apparent similarity between MCS and VS, functional imaging data show striking differences in cortical segregation and integration between these two conditions" (p. 288). Giacino, Hirsch, Schiff and Laureys (2006) suggest that in VS patients, there is a functional disconnection between the basic cortical areas and the higher cortical areas, whereas in MCS patients, fMRI studies large tracts of networks associated with language and visual processing are connected.

Owen and colleagues (2007), Coleman and colleagues (2007) and others have used PET to show that some patients with DOC react differently to others when exposed to auditory stimuli. In various studies from the Cambridge Coma Study Group, they devised tests to look at four levels of functioning in VS and MCS patients. First they asked, is there a differential response to sound versus no sound? When scanned, the brains of most patients responded differently when noise was presented compared to silence. Next, they wanted to know if there was a differential response to meaningful sentences versus noise. Fewer patients showed this pattern. The next stage involved even more complex stimuli, and the question was: is there a differential response to ambiguous versus non-ambiguous sentences? (An ambiguous sentence, for example, included words with two meanings like "dates" e.g. "there are dates in the bowl", whereas a non-ambiguous sentence did not include ambiguous words, e.g. "Brighton is a nice place to go on holiday"). Some patients appeared to show a high level of cognitive processing. However, before claiming that such patients were aware, the researchers carried out even more complex tests involving volition.

Patients were asked to imagine doing a task such as playing tennis or walking around a room. In a few patients, their responses to these tasks were indistinguishable from those of healthy control participants. Patient "G" for example, met all the criteria for VS on multidisciplinary assessments, yet the areas of the brain activated in the scanner were consistent with the areas activated in volunteers, at least for playing tennis and moving round the room. These studies led Owen and his colleagues to try to use this finding in order to communicate with DOC patients. Questions were asked of them, and they were told to imagine playing tennis if the answer was "yes" and imagine walking round the room if the answer was "no" (Owen et al., 2007; Owen & Coleman, 2008). More recently, Owen's group has found similar results using relatively more portable and less expensive electroencephalogram (EEG) technology, in which electrical activity across the scalp is measured by electrodes attached to a cap (Cruse et al., 2012).

As interesting as this research is, it is not very helpful clinically. Most of us working with VS and MCS patients want to establish a Yes/No response as soon as possible, but we cannot take people to a scanner each time. We have to work daily with these patients and their families. We need to set realistic goals such as looking at a person giving attention or tracking a moving object within a clinical situation. There is no doubt that imaging can help us understand the extent and severity of any brain injury. If we have access to research facilities and functional imaging, we might also be able to detect any residual cognitive functioning. In short, although brain scans are widely used in research, they are not always available to rehabilitation staff. In a survey of psychologists working in brain injury rehabilitation units in the United Kingdom (Wilson, Rous, & Sopena, 2008), 61% of the psychologists interviewed said they usually or always had information from CT scans; 24% usually or always had information from MRI scans; none, 0%, usually or always had access to fMRI, PET or SPECT.

Can imaging tell us much about a person's ability to function in the real world? In the Menon and colleagues (1998) study, we learned that on one task, the patient was functioning like an age-matched control subject, but the scan was not helpful for telling us what behaviours she exhibited nor for helping us plan rehabilitation. Indeed, her scan looked like that of the age-matched control. Brain scans can, indeed, identify specific lesions and areas of impaired functioning. They can tell what connections are disrupted. They can determine the severity of brain damage. They can monitor change in brain functioning over time. They can help with making decisions (e.g. surgical decisions). They can predict which people are likely to remain with persistent problems after a traumatic brain injury. It can even be therapeutic for some patients to view and have their scans explained to them (Roberts, Rafal, & Coetzer, 2006). Giacino and colleagues (2006) suggest that imaging procedures in patients with DOC may help with differential diagnosis and prognosis. They further suggest that interventions through neuromodulation may provide new opportunities for restoration of function. Bick, Mayer and Levin (2012) also suggest that fMRI and DTI may benefit clinical practice, and these are being used in neurosurgery to help brain tumour patients. There are no clear-cut benefits for rehabilitation as yet. So currently, brain scans do not help us plan rehabilitation. Meanwhile, they remain generally expensive.

If we consider imaging studies used directly in rehabilitation, we are aware that a few studies using imaging techniques to focus on 'recovery' from brain injury have been published. A word of warning is required here because it is wrong to regard *recovery* and *rehabilitation* as synonymous. They are not: rehabilitation is a process whereby people who are disabled by injury or disease work together with professional staff, relatives and members of the wider community to achieve their optimum physical, psychological, social and vocational well-being (McLellan, 1991); recovery suggests a return to a state prior to any insult to the brain – and this is, in nearly all cases, impossible to achieve.

One of the first imaging studies to look at how the brain changes after rehabilitation is by Lindgren and associates (1997). They reported changes in regional cerebral blood flow (rCBF) after cognitive rehabilitation for people who had sustained toxic encephalopathy following exposure to toxins. Later the same year, PET was used to identify the neural correlates of stimulation procedures employed in the rehabilitation of people with dysphasia (Carlomagno et al., 1997). Laatsch and colleagues (1997, 1999) used SPECT to evaluate rCBF during recovery from brain injury. She suggested that specific changes in rCBF appeared to be related both to the location of the injury and to the strategies used in cognitive rehabilitation. Continued improvements in the three patients in the 1997 study were documented in rCBF, functional abilities and cognitive skills recorded up to 45 months post insult (ibid.). A further study by Laatsch and colleagues (2004) showed that improvements following cognitive rehabilitation could be detected by fMRI scans.

In 1998, Pizzamiglio and associates used functional imaging to monitor the effects of rehabilitation for unilateral neglect. The brain regions most active after recovery were almost identical to the areas active in control participants engaged in the same tasks. This would appear to support the view that some rehabilitation methods repair the lesioned network and do not simply work through compensation or behavioural change. Jang and colleagues (2007) scanned a 25-year-old man who received comprehensive neurorehabilitation for significant problems associated with right hippocampal sclerosis, temporal lobectomy and amygdalotomy. He had 8 months of treatment, mainly for motor problems. Motor tests and fMRI were used to determine the restoration of motor function and neuro-plastic changes. The motor tests showed that the man had improved on functional reaching, grasping and hand manipulation skills. He maintained this improvement at a 6-month follow-up. An fMRI showed that before treatment, there was asymmetry of the contralesional sensori-motor cortex activation, and this was restored to normal symmetry after rehabilitation. This suggests that comprehensive neurorehabilitation may facilitate restitution of normal symmetry of cortical activation, thereby enhancing motor function. Baxter (2007) described a patient with limbic encephalitis who had severe anterograde amnesia with subsequent recovery. They used fMRI to show increased hippocampal activation before and after recovery. Scholz and associates (2009) found that training a complex visuo-spatial skill led to changes in white matter, while Thaut and McIntosh (2010) showed that music therapy led to changes in the brain as measured by brain imaging techniques. In the words of Wilde, Hunter and Bigler (2012), "Neuroimaging methods also provide insights into the complexities of brain injury, cognitive and neurobehavioural recovery" (p. 245).

While such studies employing brain imaging seem to indicate that rehabilitation can change the brain's behaviour, it remains questionable whether such imaging can help us *plan* rehabilitation. The jury is still out on this, and we can only say that some researchers *believe* this will be useful (Stinear & Ward, 2013); and some are trying to design treatments based on imaging studies (Giacino et al., 2006). It should be noted here, though, that the brain scans Gary received did not help us plan his rehabilitation programme, whereas behavioural observations were often used to work out what the problems were and how we might deal with them. In extremity, to cite a colleague, Tom Manly (personal communication), "Rehabilitation needs imaging like a fish needs a bicycle".

Chapter 4

The assault

As described by Wendie, Gary's mum, and other members of the family

.

Wendie

Gary is a father of three, two girls and a boy. He was 28 years old when he was attacked by a gang. He was always a quiet type. He didn't like his mobile phone because he thought it invaded his privacy. He liked football and supported Arsenal. He was a good father and a brave man. He liked his family around him. He worked in a bar and was good at watching what was happening. He avoided confrontation. If he thought trouble was brewing, he would go over and stop things from escalating. He worked long hours, and that

Figure 4.1 Gary as a schoolboy

was what broke his relationship up, but he saw his kids every day. He took them to school and had them every other weekend. He had a handful of good friends. Not many friends but a few close friends. I had a normal, quick birth with Gary. He was the third of five children, with two older sisters, a younger brother and a younger sister. I separated from Gary's dad, who was unemployed at the time, when Gary was 9 months old. He was an easy child. He didn't like school much. He was good at maths but hopeless at reading and writing and may have been a bit dyslexic. He had lots of friends and was popular but got up to mischief at school. For example, he hid under the tables and wouldn't come out to do his work. He left school at 16 and did several years working in electronics in different places. Then he did bar work for a while and some gardening work before he was made redundant, and then he became a carer for my Dad, who has dementia.

Zowey, Gary's younger sister

My brother was my best friend. We worked together in a pub, so for a time, he was my boss as well. He didn't like loud noises, so people had to be quiet around him, but he was great at one-liners. He was really clever at those. Gary could defuse difficult situations really quickly. He was good at this because he ran a pub. He was certainly not an aggressive type. He would just be able to get out of difficult situations. On one occasion, a man was chasing me around the pool table with a snooker cue shouting he was going to kill me, but Gary was able to calm him down straight away. Gary had never had a fight in his life.

Kelsey, Gary's firstborn, 11 years old when interviewed for this book and 8 years old when her father was attacked

Before the attack, my Dad was quiet but really funny. He did loads of funny stuff with his mates. He painted his cousin's racing car with little flowers and drove it down the road. After the attack, my mum told me that dad was in hospital, and I thought it was nothing serious. I didn't know any details until my friends at school told me it was in the newspapers.

Wendie

The day it happened, they had a barbecue in the afternoon with all the family round because it was my twin grandchildren's birthday. Gary bought the wrong coal; he bought house fire coal instead of barbecue coal and we could not get it to burn. So I had to cook the food indoors and carry it out to the garden. Everything was in a rush and we were running late. Gary left with his then partner, Donna, who was not the mother of his three children. I took the children home. When I returned home, I had had a phone call from my ex-husband to say that he was in a shop at the parade and some youths that attacked him a few months earlier had blocked him in the shop. He was too scared to leave. Gary's brother, Dean, was at my house at the time, and he said, "Right, I'll jump in the car and go up there". As Gary only lived round the corner, I rang him to say his dad was in a bit of trouble. At that time, Gary was in the bath. He jumped out of the bath and went up to the shops where his father was trapped. Dean was already there and managed to get his father out of the shop, put him in the car and took him to his flat where he was safe. As I pulled up outside my ex-husband's flat, I realised that Gary was somewhere nearby. I went to a place where the whole parade of shops could be seen and saw Gary running. I whistled (have a very loud whistle; the kids were brought up with it). Of course, Gary heard the whistle, looked over, saw me and came over. I told him that his dad was safe in his flat now.

The next minute his father was behind us. There were five youths on the corner; one of them was on a moped looking over at us. Gary's father said, "Oh, that's them". Gary said he would go and have a word with them. Gary was going to tell them to leave his Dad alone, as he could sort out tricky situations easily. I said, "No, don't even bother going over there", but Gary had gone, with his dad starting to follow. Dean had pulled up in the other car park, and I asked him to help him – to go with his brother, as there were five youths, which were too many for Gary to deal with. Dean said, "No, I'll get in the car and drive up there". I don't know why he decided to take the car, but I feel it may have saved his life. My daughter, Zowey, and her boyfriend, Luke, were there, too. I went to follow Gary, but Zowey grabbed my arm and said, "Mum, that is too far for you to walk up there, get in the car". As I walked towards the car and climbed in, some of the youths approached us with a bat. They were about to hit me and Zowey when Luke raised his arm and took the blow. I did not realise this had happened, as I was concentrating on Gary. I got in the car and drove up and round. As I was returning, Luke was sitting in the back of the car and said "There they are, there they are". I explained that I couldn't see Luke, as he was behind me, so he should not point but explain. Luke said they were in the swimming pool. I had driven past the pool, so I had to turn and go all the way back down again. I pulled up in the swimming pool car park and found Gary lying on the floor, choking. I went to him and somebody shouted "Don't move him". I said I had to move him or he would have choked. I turned him. We called the police when we were getting in the car to find Gary, as I knew there would be trouble, and we called again once we saw Gary. We waited a good while for the police and ambulance to arrive. By now there were 30 youths around. My ex-husband was lying on the ground next to Gary.

I was asked if I knew what the fight, the attack was about. I said it was over his dad. His dad is an alcoholic. He was over there drunk, and the youths had been teasing him for months. They had run over him with a moped at the beginning of the year. He was in hospital for 3 months and had pins in his knees. But the gang just targeted him. He wore bikers' gear because he was interested in all this bikers' stuff; this made him an easy target.

The police officer turned up first and then the rapid response team came. The crowds were appearing by then. After the team had worked with Gary outside on the ground, they took him into the ambulance. I went in too. The team were wondering whether to take him by air ambulance and then one said, "Oh, quick, out, get out". So I went outside. They pulled Gary back out, and I had to help hold the covers up while he was resuscitated on the ground. He had stopped breathing in the ambulance, and I assumed he was brought out as they needed extra space. When he had been resuscitated again, he was put back into the ambulance, with me and the family being transported in the back of a police car. It was so fast, we reached the hospital in seconds. The family members were given about 2 minutes to say if they wanted him to be saved. If he were saved, I remember the man saying, then he could end up being a vegetable* [note: Wendie could have been told Gary might remain vegetative; it is doubtful whether professional staff would say "vegetable"], *and would Gary want that? I said, "We are very selfish and said, 'Yeah, yeah, he would'. He wouldn't have done. He wouldn't want to be a vegetable. He would rather have died that night, wouldn't you, Gary? You would rather have died than never been able to move?"* Gary agreed with his mother and said, *"Yeah, if I couldn't move, I'd rather die".*

Wendie continued, saying, *I made the decision and had something like 2 minutes to go to say goodbye in case Gary did not survive.*

The family then had to wait for 8 hours while Gary had an operation, and he was then sent to the intensive care unit (ICU). In ICU, he was linked up to a number of machines.

Wendie continued, *The family learned to read the machines. We watched them going up and down and knew that when one dropped, we knew that meant trouble. We stayed in the hospital for a whole week in a little room. We made it our house. No one else entered. There were about eight family members during the day, with me and my ex-husband staying overnight. Donna, Gary's partner, stayed for a couple of nights.*

When it was decided to bring Gary out of ICU, he deteriorated, so he returned there for another 2 days. He then went to a ward for a further 2 days while arrangements were made for him to go to a hospital near home. He was then talking and could remember all the PINs for his mother's credit and bank cards and the number for her safe.

I said it was a good thing Gary could remember the numbers, because I couldn't! I then proceeded to enter them in my iPhone. Gary was moved to a local hospital, where, unfortunately, he had two falls which caused him to bang his head. He had to return to the London hospital where he had been treated originally and had to undergo another operation. A shunt for hydrocephalus was inserted, and Gary did not wake up for one and a half years.

His mother went on to say, *Gary could not remember the PIN numbers now.* It was explained to her that Gary had damage from the assault and damage from the shortage of oxygen when he stopped breathing. He then developed hydrocephalus, which is why he needed the shunt.

Hydrocephalus is known to retard or prevent recovery (Pickard, Coleman, & Czosnyka, 2005).

Thus, he had all sorts of things going wrong with his brain, and it was amazing to see how far he had come. Wendie agreed it was amazing and went on to share her emotions from the night the attack happened.

On that night we were all screaming, we were all . . . you know. I was shouting abuse at the crowd. I knew they were in the crowd. I knew they were in there. So, I'll get them one day. One day, I'll get them. My son, Dean, apparently, in the time of my son getting in his car, he saw Gary in the road and he said he saw one guy jump on him but Gary shrugged him off. He was dealing with it. The lad on the moped had spun off, so he chased the moped, and as the moped come up to the roundabout, the moped's gone round the wrong way. Dean came round it the correct way, and he saw the lad just come off it, he lost control of it, but he said, "I ignored him and went down" and he pulled up by the swimming pool. By now, Gary had got into the car park, and Dean said, "I saw them all on him, at least 30 of them on him, on top of him, jumping on him". Dean went to get out of the car to run to help Gary, and they turned and started running for him [Dean]. *He said, "What could I do? I had to get back in the car, Mum, I couldn't do anything". But he knocked two of them over, they couldn't get out of the way, and there was blood on his car. The youths spat on my ex-husband, they spat on Gary. My ex-husband played dead, he pretended to be dead, and they left him alone, and then the other lot attacked him as well, but he remembers that one of them turned and spat on his back. I said, "Well, what made you remember that?" He said, "Because, I remember thinking well that didn't hurt did it?" They have found the spit on them, on the jacket, but I was told that because there's too much blood on the jacket, it's ruined any chance of getting DNA. I can't understand it because John didn't . . . John didn't have any . . . the only thing John had was head injuries, so how did blood get there? I have put a formal complaint to the police about the way Gary's case was handled, and I am complaining about it. We had a young girl that was at one of the clubs and the girlfriends heard the boys bragging up there, how they kicked him, they did this, they did that, and this girl said, "Why, you know this was Gary Hayward? If you know, you should be going forward". "Oh, you shut up", he said, "or we're going to get them up here and we'll do the same to you".*

The attack had been featured on *Crimewatch*, a BBC television programme which attempts to catch criminals. Wendie was asked whether anything had come of the *Crimewatch* programme. *No,* said Wendie, *somebody else offered to double the reward. We had a couple of young girls that privately mailed me and they said that they knew who did it and who do they talk to? They rang* Crimewatch *but no one got back to us.*

Within an hour of the attack, 30 names were given to me. People were phoning me. I believe I know who did it. I gave the names to the police. I was phoned to say that one of the alleged main attackers [name withheld here] *ran through the housing estate shouting, "I've killed a man, I've killed a man". A couple of minutes later, I received another call from somebody who did not know the previous caller saying exactly the same thing. So I believe the boy must have been seen running through the estate doing this. Then there was an email from a young girl saying that she had heard about it. She knew who did it. The police went round to her house, and because she was not in, they left a note to say she should contact them. I went back to the police to ask if they had spoken to her. I was told they had not, as she had not contacted them. I thought they should have sent a warrant and was told that they do not do this any more and I had been watching too much television! Yet another person* gave me the name of the boy who had been shouting he had killed a man. One boy who did get arrested that night was the one that hit Luke. He was arrested because Luke recognised him. Later when the case went to court, the man was fined £25.

So Luke received £25 compensation. The mother of that boy saw Luke's mother in a shop, grabbed my arm and said, "Your son owes me £25. I want it back". But one of the young girls who named the man who did it ran into the arms of the man's sister that night. She had blood all over her and she said if the police interviewed her she would admit who did it. They did not interview her. It made me feel that they did not want to know. My ex-husband's camera was stolen that night. It was in his pocket, and he had filmed some of the activity beforehand when he had been abused outside the shop. Obviously the camera was stolen. I was told the address where the camera was being held and informed the police. On the night of Gary's attack, while waiting for Gary to come out of the operating theatre, I was told where the camera was.

I heard rumours that there was a knife at the scene. It was never picked up. The night before Gary's attack, two lads on a tram were attacked. A good few of the 30 people who had attacked Gary were believed to be involved in the tram attack. There was video evidence of that attack, and they did go to court. They thought there was to be a reprisal the night after the tram attack. In anticipation of this big fight, they had a car with weapons ready in the car. Then they took the weapons from the car to use on Gary instead. After Gary's attack, I was told that the car had been impounded. A year later, a new officer was put in charge of the case. There was a meeting during which I asked about the impounded car. The new man in charge said, "What car?" and I said, "The car what was impounded". I said, "It was X's car [name withheld], it was impounded because it had the weapons in it the night Gary was attacked". When I went to any meetings, I took other people with me, as they were all interested in what the police had to say. There were always eight or nine people. But now the car seems to have disappeared.

Wendie feels there will be some kind of justice one day.

I know that Gary is very popular. I have been told, "Wendie, we will get them", and I say, "Oh, leave it, let the police deal with it". I feel that one day the perpetrators will be charged with Gary's attack. It is a matter of time. They will upset a girlfriend because they all brag. They'll upset a girlfriend and that girlfriend will go to the police. It doesn't matter when.

Even the local newspaper was not allowed to print the story. They tried to link the tram attack with Gary's attack. The tram attack had not gone to court at that time because it had only just happened. The people in the tram attack did all go to court. Same people, same names, but they walked away! Nothing was done. Since then, a few of them have attacked other people. One girl was assaulted in a park. This particular lad who is in the paper frequently still gets away with it.

Wendie knows that at this stage, she cannot name names even though some people, including reporters, say "give us the names". She believes that the Stephen Lawrence case came together because names were leaked in the paper. She told us, *"I've still got to give the police a chance and see what happens"*. She has gone to the ombudsman and is waiting for them to contact her. If nothing happens, then she says that eventually she will give names to the press but has to do this when she is ready. She feels that if she does this too soon, she may lose the case in court. Gary was attacked in October 2011 and, at the time of writing this section (December 2014), there has been no charge.

Zowey's diary

Zowey kept a diary and a scrapbook recording the assault and what happened in the following months. Mostly this agrees with Wendie's account, although some details are different. The main point to make is that Zowey's diary is written very close to the time everything happened. Her first entry was October 2, 2011, the day after the attack.

The barbecue did not go to plan, as Gary had brought the wrong coal. Gary and Donna left about five thirty p.m. John, Gary's dad, left soon after and I left with Dean. John rang Wendie about eight p.m. saying that the gang of kids who had troubled him before were causing trouble again. Wendie rang Gary while Dean rushed to get to John. Meanwhile, me and my partner Luke and Wendie went by car to look for John. On the way, we saw Gary walking to the parade, but he did not hear us calling. We parked the car outside John's flat and found Dean, who said his father was safe inside his flat. Then John appeared and pointed to the kids, saying that was them. So Gary shouted over to them to leave John alone. Some lads went further off and kept telling Gary to come, to come, to come. They lured him to where the fighting was. There was Gary and three of the youths. One of them threw a punch at Gary, so Gary hit back. Luke went to chase after Gary but saw some boys walking towards me and my mum, so Luke went back to make sure the boys went for him instead. One of them had a pole in his hand and hit Luke with it, but Luke managed to put his arm up and protect himself. Wendie, Luke and I jumped in the car to find Gary but lost him. Meanwhile, I was telephoning the police. When we arrived back at the parade, everything was quiet. We drove to the swimming pool car park, and that is where we found Gary. John was by his side. We tried to keep Gary as still as possible until the police arrived.

I got out of the car and ran over to my brother. At first I thought he was all right and was going to say, "oh, just give me a minute" just as he had done at other times when he wasn't feeling too good. He would say, "Just leave me alone, I'll get up in my own time". I thought he was going to be fine, but instead he was making weird noises. Nevertheless, I believed that he knew we were there because he was holding my hand, he even squeezed my hand. When my mother arrived, she was hysterical. By then there was a big crowd around, and in that crowd were the kids who had attacked Gary. They had come back to look at what they had done.

I thought there were 30 people involved, but I didn't think every single one of them attacked my brother. They were just watching. There were five or six main people who actually attacked Gary. From what we could gather, it was the main five. People told us they saw them hit Gary with this and with that. The others were there, but they didn't touch him. I think if all 30 of them had attacked him, he would have died.

For some reason, people in Addington are just scared of this group of boys. They were about 16 or 17 years old. Even knowing what they did to Gary, I'm still not scared of them. I still tell them what I think of them in the street. I just have this idea that you shouldn't be scared of anybody. No one has the right to scare you, but the fact that they were all standing in the crowd and we knew they were and we kept saying to them they're in the crowd, go and have a look at their T-shirts, they have blood on them. I think at that stage, the police thought it was just a brawl, gang on gang, and they didn't care that much. They probably see it day in day out, and they just thought "why should we care really?" The paramedics worked on Gary for over an hour, and all the rest of us could do was pray Gary would be all right. He died three times that night and the paramedics brought him round.

Zowey said that Gary was then taken to Kings College hospital, where he had a scan which identified a blood clot on the brain. The family was told that Gary needed emergency surgery to remove the clot. They heard that he had a slim chance of surviving the operation but no chance of surviving without it. Zowey said, *I didn't think he was going to die. I just didn't, but I was scared that he was, but in my heart of hearts I didn't actually think he would die.*

Gary was taken for surgery about eleven p.m. While he was there, the police took statements from the family who found out that one of the kids was [name withheld], the one who had attacked Luke. Luke recognised him. Then there was an agonising wait until about seven a.m., when Gary was sent to the critical care unit. The operation had gone well, but part of Gary's skull had been removed due to swelling of the brain. Gary was in a coma and had been sedated. The family were told that the first 48 hours were critical. They stayed at the hospital, as they could not bear to leave Gary.

Chapter 5

Early days in hospital

On October 3, the day after Gary's surgery, Zowey wrote in her diary:

Today we have not left your side. Only two people are allowed at your bedside at any one time so we took turns to see you. It was really hard, Gaz, because we knew it was you but you didn't look like you anymore; you had wires everywhere. There are two images I will never get out of my head. The first is when I found you and the second is when you were in that coma because it is the first time I felt helpless. Not being able to help you is the worst feeling in the world. All we could do was talk to you and hold your hand. We still have your blood on our clothes. We haven't slept and we haven't eaten. I was supposed to get Jamie [Zowey's son] back today but Luke's dad is keeping him until Wednesday so we can be with you. The story of what happened is now on the internet in Croydon.

The Internet report was by Joanna Till, a journalist with the *Croydon Advertiser*, who wrote (Thursday, October 13, 2011), "A young man is fighting for his life in hospital after an incident in New Addington last night (Sunday). The victim who is understood to be 26, is in a critical but stable condition after a brawl in Central Parade at about 8.45 p.m. A Metropolitan Police spokesman confirmed officers were called to the scene after reports of men fighting. A 58 year old man, understood to be the young man's father, was also rushed to hospital where he is said to be in a stable condition. No one has been arrested in connection with the incident. An eye witness, who asked not to be named, said she was driving along Central Parade when she saw a group of boys aged between 17 and 20 running towards the swimming pool car park. 'There must have been 30 of them' she said. 'There was a lot of shouting and swearing and the next minute I saw them using wooden bats and metal poles to beat up two men. It all happened so quickly. After a few minutes they ran off. They must have heard the sirens'. The woman said she stopped her car to attend to the two men, who were on the ground. She said the younger man, who she believed to be 26, was unconscious and covered in blood. 'The older man managed to raise his head and asked me to check his son to see if he was still breathing' she added. 'Even though the dad didn't look too good he was more concerned about his son'.

A spokesman for London Ambulance Service confirmed it had sent a single responder in a car to the scene, along with two ambulance crews and the air ambulance doctor in a car. Paramedics spent more than an hour treating the younger man at the scene before rushing him to Kings College Hospital in Denmark Hill as a priority. His condition had improved slightly by Monday afternoon to 'critical but stable'". The report ended with two updates: 'Victim Gary Hayward was defending his father from bullies' and: 'Arrests have been made in connection with the attack.'

The following day, Zowey wrote:

There is still no change, not only did we steal the relative's room all night we also stole it all day. We still haven't slept! Luke and I did our statements today. It's really weird because the time goes so fast. We thought it would go really slow but it doesn't. . . although when we have to come out so someone else can see you it goes slow because we want to get back in there to see you! We stayed in the relative's room overnight again but as we are now not allowed to see you overnight we tried to get some sleep. Luke fell asleep but I couldn't because every time I close my eyes I see you lying on the floor. I got up to go for a cigarette but I got lost so I had to ring Luke to come and rescue me at about 3 in the morning.

Figure 5.1 Early days in hospital

I am really missing you, Gary. I really can't function without you. If you die, a part of me will die with you. You are the person I am closest to because you understand me like I understand you. It will really devastate me, Gary, so wake up!

On October 5, Zowey wrote that they were given more names of the people who had attacked Gary and passed these on to the police. She said:

You still haven't woken up, Gaz but you are really starting to heal now. If we look at your nose and part of your eyes we can see the Gary we know and love again. She explained that she had to leave the hospital to be with her son, Jamie, which was one of the hardest things she had ever had to do. *I was convinced that if I left something bad would happen.* She went on to say that rumours were flying round on Facebook that Gary had been stabbed and had died.

There were further updates posted online about Gary on October 5:

Two teenagers have been arrested in connection with the attack. A 17 year old was arrested on October 3 on suspicion of GBH and attempted murder and has been bailed until November 4. Another 17 year old was arrested the following day on suspicion of GBH and attempted murder and has been bailed until November 24; he was also charged with common assault and possession of an offensive weapon in relation to a separate incident in Central Parade on the same night. He appeared at Croydon Youth Court on Wednesday and was bailed until November 4. Anyone with information about the assault is asked to call Croydon CID.

On Saturday, October 8, Gary started to come off sedation. Zowey wrote in her diary:

I can't wait for you to start sitting up and chatting. There is a bit of bad news though. We found out that you are blind in your left eye as your nerve that makes you see is dead and there is so much blood behind your other eye they cannot tell if there is anything wrong with it. Once you are better they will give you an operation to remove the blood.

The following day, 1 week after the attack, Zowey noted that Gary was starting to open his eyes. She wrote, *You have no idea how happy I am, Gaz, you are just amazing. The swelling on your face has gone down and you look like Gary again!*

The day after that, Gary was squeezing the hands of his family members. Zowey wrote, *We thought you would be paralysed down your right side but you are moving it all. We are all just willing you to wake up now.*

John Ling, a clinical nurse specialist for survivors of brain injury, was working closely with Gary's neurosurgeon and overseeing Gary's progress. On October 11, John Ling gave the family a booklet about head injuries and the recovery process. The book suggested that it could take a year for Gary to get better (in fact, the recovery process can go on for many years). John thought that Gary might have to learn to talk, walk and remember all over again. Later, in an interview, Zowey commented, *"We sat in a meeting with several top neurologists and they said, 'It will probably be a few months before Gary's ready to talk. That is if he comes out of coma'. At that point we were still at that stage of IF he comes out of coma. They gave us these leaflets about him learning to read, write, talk and walk everything. They said he could be paralysed. They said it would be a few years for him to get back to normal and he could still be left with quite severe brain damage. We thought, 'Oh, my god, it would be evil if he had to live like that. We'd made the wrong decision, letting him have that operation'"*.

Zowey felt that doctors always told people the worst news. She wanted Gary to wake up and prove them all wrong. She wrote in her diary:

They don't know you like we do. We know you are a fighter and nothing is going to stop you walking out of there. We were also told that once you get better you would most likely go to rehab to learn things again with people your age and who have the same injuries as you. I think that would be a good thing as you will be with people you can talk to about things and make some new friends.

Later she told us, *And then, within a week, he was talking and he had everything there. He could tell who everybody was. He was sitting up in bed and chatting away. Then he was moved to Farnborough and he was saying "I want to go home". We said "You can't go home until you can walk". So he said "Well get me up and walk" and he was walking with two people and up and down the stairs. We couldn't believe it.*

Zowey's diary continued with news that on October 12, Luke saw a picture of [name withheld] and recognised him as one of the boys who jumped on Gary's back the night of the attack. She said the police wanted Luke to go to a lineup, and if he managed to point him out, the boy might be charged. Gary's father was asked to attend a lineup too, but said he would not recognise him. Zowey also noted that Gary had been moved farther away from the nurses' station, which meant he was not in so much danger. *But,* she wrote, *you are starting to pull out your wires so the nurses are thinking about putting mittens on your hands to stop you! I knew you would hate having the wires in. I keep getting scared you are going to hurt yourself if you keep pulling at them.*

The day after that, October 13, Gary started to talk. He was very quiet, though, and could barely be heard. The family felt this was not surprising given he had had tubes down his throat. *You even remembered us,* wrote Zowey, *you asked where Jamie was and where your kids were. I have said this before but you are Amazing!*

Two weeks after the attack, Gary was tired and not himself, but he was making the family laugh again. Zowey felt he was not himself because he told her to go away, and she felt the old Gary would never have said that to her. She noted that he had trouble remembering things, but they were just so happy Gary was awake and she was proud to have him as her brother. He continued to improve over the next few days. On October 20, the doctor told Wendie that he was very impressed with Gary and now expected him to make a full recovery. He was, of course, still blind in one eye, but there was hope that he could be cured. This was the day Gary finally recognised Zowey but called Donna, his partner, Laura (he does not know anyone called Laura). This continued the following day, when there were problems with Gary toileting. He kept wanting to go and tried to get out of bed to find a toilet. The family explained to him that he had a catheter on, but Gary seemed not to believe them. He kept saying he wanted to leave hospital. Zowey wrote that Gary was

A little bit depressed at the thought of having to stay in hospital for a while but that is a stage we have been told you are going to go through. The next stage is for him to get angry and upset which I am not looking forward to but we will be there no matter what. Even if you shout at us, you are not getting rid of us that easy!

Although Gary continued to be depressed about having to stay in hospital, he carried on improving. He started to eat and drink on his own instead of being fed through a tube. At the end of October, he asked the nurses to call his mother, as he did not think she knew he was in hospital. On November 1 at about 8.30 in the evening, Gary was transferred to the Princess Royal Hospital nearer to his home. Zowey wrote, *I think it is really good as the doctors at Kings now say they are over qualified to treat you. This means you are on the mend.*

Gary stayed at the Princess Royal for a while. On November 9, Zowey told him, *"I think you are in the next stage of recovery now – the ANGRY stage. I think it is getting to you that we are all fussing over you as every time you need the toilet we walk you there or if you want to sit in your chair we hold on to you. Remember, it is because we all care. It doesn't matter how much you shout at us we will still be helping you".*

The next day, Zowey decided to stop the diary. She wrote, *You are doing so well now, Gary, I think I can stop this diary for you as you are more than capable at remembering it all. I'm really proud of you, Gary, keep up the good work. Love you lots.*

However, she restarted the diary on Monday, November 28, saying, *Hey, Gaz, I'm back. You had a bit of a setback. You fell out of bed a few days ago because you got up on your own in the early hours of the morning to go to the toilet but your bed sheets got tangled around your foot so you fell. You seemed OK at first but then you started to get confused about things. You called Jamie a brat and said you hated him and you thought you were pregnant with a fish! We kept telling the nurses that your head wasn't as sunken in as usual but they weren't worried. It was only when it got to this morning that they were a little worried and took you down for a scan. They found that you had water on the brain* [hydrocephalus] *so you were rushed back to King's. When you arrived there we couldn't even get a conversation from you, you were scared and confused and kept lashing out at everyone. You didn't know who any of us were. The doctors came down and said they were going to put a shunt in your head to drain the fluid from your brain. It is not life threatening because you haven't got a skull* [part of Gary's skull was removed during the surgery, as his brain was swelling; this meant any swelling as a result of the hydrocephalus would not be restricted by bone] *and it is perfectly safe to leave it until tomorrow morning. Mum managed to get you calm and fall asleep for the night.*

In a later interview, when asked about the fall, Zowey said, *"He was in bed and he had a bottle to go to the toilet but he filled it up. He even started drinking his old drink and filling his drink bottles up, but the nurses never came in. He kept pushing the button and they never came. Now Gary is very proud. At work, he would not use the toilets if anybody was in there. He would wait until they had gone. He is very private. So he thought, 'Well I HAVE walked, so I'll get up' and he did but he got his feet caught in the sheet and he fell. He said he did not hit his head. He was adamant about that and told mum the next day. He said, 'Mum, you're going to ground me because I fell out of bed but I needed the toilet'. So Mum went on the rampage outside, having a go at everybody. The nurses said that they could not be there 24/7 but they would put a mattress down. Gary swore he never hit his head, so, of course, the next night they did not put a mattress down and he fell out of the bed again. The next day or the day after, he started going downhill. We also noticed that when mum was getting him to push the help button, no one would come. Then one day she persuaded him to press the help button again.*

There was no noise whatsoever. Then my mum went out there and went mad at them. Gary has had a rough ride".

The following day, Gary should have left the Princess Royal Hospital to go to a rehabilitation centre but, instead, he was having his operation. Zowey's diary entry for that day said:

I am so gutted for you, Gaz, but I know you are going to be OK. The operation only took an hour or two and then we came up to visit you but you were fast asleep. The doctor said, as soon as the sedation wears off you will be as right as rain again. We made sure you were settled and then left so you could rest. See you tomorrow, Gaz.

But the next day Gary still had not woken. After a few hours, Wendie and Zowey asked the doctors to look at Gary. They were told that it just takes time and that the sedation could take an hour to wear off on some people and even a week on others. In fact, Gary remained asleep for many months.

Then in early December he started shaking violently. There was concern it might be blood poisoning or epilepsy. He went back to the high dependency unit and had another scan, which suggested the shunt was not working properly. Another shunt was inserted. On December 13, the doctors thought the new shunt was satisfactory and that Gary was looking a little more alert, so they were hoping he would wake soon. Although the family wanted him to wake for his birthday on December 17, Gary did not wake. They hoped he would wake for Christmas, but he did not. On December 27, a nurse and a patient said Gary had smiled and had lifted his left arm. On the 29th, he was reported to have been crying and moaning, and on the 30th, Wendie was cuddling Gary when he lifted his arm and held her elbow. On the last day of 2011, Gary was fidgeting but not really conscious. He was moved to the Raphael Medical Centre on February 13, 2012, where he remained in a state of low awareness for more than a year until April 2013, more than 19 months after the attack.

Zowey was asked how it came about that Gary was admitted to the Raphael Medical Centre. She said, *"They came looking for Gary. They came looking for him. We were sitting with him one day. We had only just started discussing rehabilitation. At this point we were not sure if he was ever going to wake up again. We said there was no way he was going to go in a home because that was one of the choices offered to us. We said, 'He's not going into a home'. We were saying that maybe we could get him into rehabilitation because someone had mentioned Blackheath so we thought that maybe we could get him there. The next thing there was a knock on the door and this man said, 'I'm from the Raphael Medical Centre in Tonbridge'. I don't know how they knew about Gary. They were just coming in looking for him. My mum and I thought someone up there was watching – one of Gary's best friends died a few years before. A shiver came down on us. We felt that she* [the best friend who had died] *sent the man from the Raphael here. It was like the grace of God that he came. We just could not believe it. He came at a really dark time because we were frightened so much because nobody had any hope for Gary. It was only us that had the hope and we were drastically losing it. Everyone was saying, 'No, put him in a home, he would be better off in a home'. We said, 'OK, we'll take him home. We won't put him in a home, no, we'll take him home'. So, yes, it was nice of that bloke to come in and actually believe in Gary because he was coming with so much confidence. It was just amazing. We couldn't believe it. We did want him to come to the Raphael, we snapped it up straight away. Because one, it was closer than any of the other places and then when mum come to view it she said, 'Yes, we definitely want him there'. Don't get me wrong, when we first came here and after Gary had been there for a few weeks, we thought, 'Have we made the right decision?' That was because it seemed pretty – erm – I don't want to say hippy like – well a bit different – so we were thinking 'what are we doing? What are we doing to Gary?' but it works, it works"!*

With Gary's permission, the discharge notes from Kings College Hospital were obtained. As we know, Gary was admitted to the hospital on October 2 and to the intensive care unit on October 3, 2011 after his operation. He was discharged on October 20. The primary diagnosis was left-sided acute subdural hematoma (a blood clot). He sustained a subarachnoid haemorrhage (bleeding into the surface area of the brain) and facial and skull fractures due to an assault by a baseball bat on October 2, 2011. A left craniotomy was carried out. He had a fixed midsized left pupil on arrival and was found to have many fractures to his facial bones. Conservative management of his fractures was recommended. There was a leak of cerebral spinal fluid from his nose, but this subsided. The breathing tube was removed, and Gary maintained a Glasgow Coma Scale score of 10 (eye opening 4, verbal response 1 and motor response 5). This meant that he opened his eyes spontaneously, there was no verbal response and he made a motor response by localising to pain.

On October 20, 2011, Gary was transferred to a specialist rehabilitation unit. The discharge summary repeated the medical information and noted that Gary had a very supportive mother. It said that Gary had been fully independent prior to the assault and was a carer for his grandfather. The assessment report said Gary's motor skills could not be formally assessed, but he had a full range of movement when his limbs were passively moved, and he was moving all four limbs spontaneously. It was not possible to formally assess his sensation. Visually, his left eye was swollen and half shut, while there were sporadic movements in his right eye, which did not focus. He appeared to be oriented to person but not to place, time or situation. He was thought to be in post-traumatic amnesia (the period of confusion following coma). He was able to follow single-stage verbal commands but not consistently. He made some attempts at mouthing but was not comprehensible. Because of his low level of alertness, a swallowing assessment was not considered advisable. He was, however, able to eat and drink a normal diet and fluids despite requiring encouragement to eat.

In summary, Gary was noted to have significant motor, visual, cognitive and communication deficits impacting on his ability to participate in functional tasks. He was beginning to show improvement in these areas, and therefore it was felt he would benefit from a period of intensive specialist neurological rehabilitation with the aim to increase his functional independence.

Gary was discharged to the Princess Royal University Hospital on November 1, 2011, having been accepted at Blackheath Neurological Rehabilitation Unit. He was due to be transferred on November 9, but his condition deteriorated. He had another CT scan and was found to have hydrocephalus. Consequently, he was readmitted to Kings College Hospital on November 23, 2011, for the insertion of a shunt and a valve. He was slow to recover from surgery, was only localising to painful stimuli and had developed a left-sided tremor. When he was assessed in neurology, this was assumed to be a seizure, which was treated with antiepileptic medication and antibiotics. His scalp became sunken; this was thought to be due to the shunt over-draining the fluid; hence the shunt was tied. This resulted in Gary becoming somewhat more alert. However, the hydrocephalus progressed, and he deteriorated again. Then the shunt was untied and a programmable valve placed in the shunt. Post-operatively there was no improvement. He was discharged back to the Princess Royal for further rehabilitation. At this point, Gary's eyes opened spontaneously. He was localising to pain and had a left-sided tremor. He was not communicating and showed no evidence of comprehension. His family was told that neurological improvement would be slow and unpredictable.

In March 2012, Gary's shunt was reviewed, as there was marked depression in the left parietal region. He was noted to be wheelchair bound, with minimal motor function and no verbalisation. In August 2012, Gary went back to Kings College for the cranioplasty. This was reported to be an uncomplicated procedure.

Chapter 6

Admission to the Raphael Medical Centre

The Raphael Medical Centre (RMC) is a unique, independent hospital, specialising in the neurorehabilitation of adults. The philosophy, based on Rudolf Steiner's principles, follows an approach which believes in the integration of mind, body and spirit. It is used in a number of fields including agriculture, teaching, arts and medicine. In rehabilitation, it is used to support people suffering from complex neurological disabilities including physical, cognitive and behavioural impairments. Otherwise known as anthroposophic medicine (AM), it complements and is integrated with mainstream medicine. Although Ernst (2004) found no randomised control trials evaluating AM in its entirety, Kienle, Kienle and Albonico (2006) conducted a systematic review and concluded that "Trials of varying design and quality in a variety of diseases predominantly describe good clinical outcome for AM, little side effects, high satisfaction of patients and presumably slightly less costs" (p. 7). Although some rehabilitation professionals may remain sceptical about the effectiveness of some components of AM practised at the centre, it should be pointed out that much of the therapy offered there – and indeed described in this book – is of the scientific kind practised throughout the rehabilitation centres in the United Kingdom. What is certain is that the standard of care at the centre is very good overall, and compassion for the patients is there for all to see. The service at the centre is no more expensive than the National Health Service (NHS), and staff do not give up on the patients. This means rehabilitation can be provided for much longer than would normally be the case in most other units offering rehabilitation to brain-injured people. Most of the patients at the centre are paid for by the NHS. Indeed, most have been treated in NHS facilities for several weeks or months before being referred on to other services such as the Raphael, who take patients who are regarded as difficult to place because of their serious conditions.

Practitioners employ a variety of treatment techniques including massage, exercise, counselling and the use of anthroposophic medicines and remedies which are similar to homeopathic remedies. Thus, some of the therapies are unlike those found in more traditional hospitals and rehabilitation services. This includes, for example, neuro-functional re-organisation or the Padovan method. This was developed in Brazil by Mrs Beatriz Padovan, a speech pathologist (Padovan, 1992), and is based on neurodevelopmental principles and described more fully in the following chapter. It was stimulated by the studies of the educationalist, Rudolf Steiner, and on the developmental psychologist Piaget's observations on sensorimotor intelligence. This method is used in rehabilitation to attempt to use the developmental sequence to teach people how to use both their bodies (such as in walking, manipulating objects, swallowing and talking) and their brains (for affective, perceptual and cognitive functions) again. The views of Nudo (2013) would concur with this; he believes that recovery after brain injury has parallels to the activity seen during normal brain development.

Gary came to the Raphael 4 months after the assault and immediately began the integrative multisensory interventions. The multi-disciplinary team included doctors, nurses, occupational therapists, physiotherapists, an art therapist, a music therapist, a neuropsychologist, speech and language therapists, a dietician and neuro-functional re-organisation therapist. Initial assessments on admission showed that Gary had a flaccid (limp) tone in all four limbs; he had no control of his neck and trunk muscles and was completely dependent on the rehabilitation assistants for his daily living activities such as bathing, dressing, toileting and so forth. He received all nutrition through a percutaneous endoscopic gastrostomy (PEG) tube, which is considered to be preferable to a nasogastric tube (Andrews, 2005). He remained in a vegetative state for more than 13 months and then progressed to a minimally conscious state for a further 4 months before regaining consciousness.

Initial information gathering and intervention during the early days at the RMC

Gary's brain injury affected him in many ways. He was on anti-convulsants and antibiotics to combat his epilepsy and his frequent urinary infections. He had a high temperature and a fast heartbeat; he was unable to talk; and the muscle tone in all his extremities as well as his head and neck was poor. He was unable to sit without support and required trunk and head support at all times. He had to be restrained for his safety using a seatbelt while positioned in a wheelchair, and bedrails were in place while he was in bed. He was receiving total assistance for all his daily care, bed mobility and transfers. A number of factors could be contributing to his low level of consciousness, including medications, infections and the neurological condition of his brain. He was regularly reviewed by neuro consultants to evaluate the effectiveness of medications, especially the anti-convulsants he was receiving for his epilepsy. Gary's brain injury affected all his family, both practically and emotionally: they were devastated by his situation; and of course their roles and routines were changed because of their frequent visits to the RMC to see Gary.

Gary's occupational therapist, Samira, began Gary's first session by interviewing the family members, especially his caring mother, Wendie, and his sister, Zowey, to discover information about Gary's interests and valued activities, roles and routines. This information was needed so it could be incorporated into therapy plans. The family described Gary as an active young man whose nickname was Gaz. He used to work as a bar steward prior to the assault. He enjoyed playing the guitar and his favourite musical group was Queen. According to his mother, Gary's favourite holiday destination was Brighton. Although he was single, he had a partner, Donna, and had been with another partner before who was the mother of his three children. Before the assault, he saw his children almost every day. He was very close to his mother, his sister and his children. He was not choosy about his food and drinks; however, beer and chicken were his favourites.

As Gary was still in a vegetative state, his therapist's first goal to aid possible rehabilitation was to provide an enriched environment that would begin to orient him to the external rhythm and structure of everyday life. Samira developed a programme of environmental stimulation using the information provided by his family, including his favourite music, pictures of family members and varied sensory stimulations such as stimulating his olfactory senses through the presentation of mustard seed oil. Nursing staff and family members were taught how to position Gary most effectively and how to provide environmental stimulation. A book was kept for family members to document any observed behaviour: for example, opening his eyes when Zowey called his name and following his children with his eyes when they were moving or talking.

At this stage, Gary's responses were noted to be reflexive, that is to say non-purposeful in nature. He was opening his eyes with or without stimulation, thus maintaining a sleep–wake cycle. This meant he was out of coma but showing no response to environmental stimuli. At first, he did not respond to any sensory stimuli except pain. He was unresponsive to visual threat (fingers moving towards his eyes) and showed no visual or auditory startle responses. When a light was shone into his eyes, his right pupil reacted, but the left pupil remained fixed with no reaction. Although Gary responded to olfactory and gustatory stimulation, responses were, once again, reflexive in nature. Thus, he pumped his lips and showed delayed swallowing, biting, chewing and tightening of his lips. His responses to sensory stimulations were regularly observed and recorded on the Wessex Head Injury Matrix (WHIM) by Barbara, the neuropsychologist, and Samira (see Chapter 7 for these results).

To minimise the chances of pressure sores, Gary was provided with a pressure-reduction foam modular mattress and a profiling bed (one that allows changes to different parts of the body such as raising the legs or the head independently). Two rehabilitation assistants turned Gary every 2 hours to relieve pressure when he was in bed. Nurses and rehabilitation assistants play an integral part in the interdisciplinary team at the RMC, helping restore each patient's health to the optimum level. In addition, these helpers acted as mediators in communicating Gary's current status to his family members and to other members of the team. Thus, doctors were regularly informed of any changes in Gary's heart rate, blood pressure and other vital signs; the occupational therapists were informed of changes in cognition or behaviour; the physiotherapists were told about any mobility issues or any soreness resulting from the splints used to reduce contractures; and the speech and language therapist was kept informed about the swallowing chart. The nurses and assistants were able to ensure procedures to maintain goals set by the team were implemented. They communicated with the respective disciplines in order to facilitate adjustments in the management of Gary's rehabilitation programme. On admission, the Waterlow Scale for measuring the risk of developing pressures sores was administered to Gary. His score of 21 suggested he was at high risk of developing a pressure sore. However, due to the procedures outlined for positioning and turning, Gary did not develop any pressure sores. The nursing assessments and care plans were carefully followed.

Because of the nature of the problems Gary experienced from his brain injury, the physiotherapists and occupational therapists used the biomechanical and cognitive perceptual models to guide much of the therapy. The biomechanical frame of reference is used to treat patients with activity limitations due to impairments in biomechanical body structures and functions, including structural instability, decreased strength, limited range of motion and poor endurance. Treatment within the biomechanical frame of reference focuses on preventing or decreasing impairments through the use of activity and exercises (James, 2003). In the cognitive perceptual framework, learning is defined as an interaction between task and environment. The application of this approach involves specifying strategies for more effective learning through task analysis to (i) inform the transfer of learned skills or behaviours; (ii) apply learned skills or strategies to different environments and tasks; (iii) develop self-monitoring for the application and proper utilisation of strategies; and (iv) use motivation or active participation and awareness to drive further learning (Roberts, 2005).

Intervention was adjusted to Gary's performance capacity throughout his rehabilitation, and secondary complications were avoided. Gary received regular passive mobilisation, and his muscle tone was frequently monitored to prevent the development of any contractures or deformities. He received assistance from two staff for all his transfers using a hoist. To reduce any obstruction to his airways and to improve the amount of air getting into his lungs, his chest was examined daily, followed, when necessary, by chest clearance exercises from one of the physiotherapists. In the long term, this also helped reduce the frequency of chest infections. An upright posture was important to enhance alertness, to stimulate weight bearing and to stretch hamstrings. This was not easy to accomplish on a standing frame because of Gary's low awareness state, but he regularly used the tilt table to maximum benefits. A tilt table is a mechanical or electrical table designed to elevate patients from a horizontal to a vertical position in a controlled, incremental manner. It is used when patients do not have enough muscle tone to manage an upright posture. A standing frame, on the other hand, can be used when muscle tone improves. Some of the advantages of placing patients in an upright stance include the following: It enables the stretching of hip flexors, knee flexors and ankle plantar flexors; patients can begin to control their head and neck; and there is gradual weight bearing of one or both lower extremities. Wilson, Dhamapurkar, Tunnard, Watson and Florschutz (2013) show that more behaviours are observed when patients are assessed in the upright position.

Soon Gary began receiving regular mat exercises. Here the focus was on re-learning a sequential developmental pattern based on Padovan's approach of neuro-functional re-organisation therapy (Padovan, 1992). The sequences began with homo-lateral (movement on one side) and cross-lateral (movement on both sides) patterns of his arms and legs followed by rolling, hand exercises and finally oral exercises working on oral reflexes. He responded to these stimulations with inconsistent swallowing, sometimes pumping his lips and sometimes not. He usually had difficulty swallowing his saliva. Gary's nasolabial folds (smile lines) were asymmetrical; his chewing and frowning were more noticeable on the left side. This was because he had more problems with the right side of his face due to the fact that the left brain hemisphere sustained more damage during the assault.

To maximise Gary's level of alertness, enhance his social participation and prevent him from being deprived of sensory stimulations, he also received art and music therapy sessions with hand-over-hand support from the therapists (see Chapter 10 for a fuller account of his music therapy). Even though Gary was in a low awareness state, he was introduced to the guitar and his hands moved over this, as he had enjoyed this activity prior to his brain injury. As well as these therapies, Gary received embrocation treatments using special oils.

The speech and language therapist assessed Gary to determine his swallowing capacity and to see if there was a way to communicate with him. He showed no changes in his facial expression except in response to pain. A true assessment of his comprehension and expressive language was difficult due to his limited responses. Responses often noticed were reflexive in nature, such as tongue pumping followed by reflexive swallowing.

Further details of assessments over the next few months when Gary was vegetative and minimally conscious can be found in Chapter 7, while details of assessments after he regained consciousness can be found in Chapter 9.

Chapter 7

Assessments while Gary was vegetative and minimally conscious

Recovery from brain injury is a long-term process spanning many years of a person's life. Patients who remain in a vegetative or minimally conscious state following profound brain injury present with a complex picture of physical, cognitive and emotional disturbances and, in this respect, Gary was not exceptional. Following severe brain injury, many patients progress through stages of coma, VS and MCS as they emerge into a state of full awareness. Some will remain in a vegetative or minimally conscious state for the rest of their lives (RCP, 2013, p. 1). Gary remained in a vegetative state for nearly 15 months and in a minimally conscious state for a further few months. To have done so well after this lengthy period is not only exceptional, but in most of the published cases, it is rare to have such detailed documentation of the recovery process.

Due to his devastating brain injury, Gary lacked the mental capacity to make decisions about his own care and treatment. So all decisions were taken for him on the basis of what was in his best interests. Accurate diagnosis using skilled assessment is essential for clinical decision making and appropriate treatment planning (Royal College of Physicians, 2013, p. 14). Gary was regularly assessed with two measures typically used to monitor people who are in coma, the vegetative state or the minimally conscious state. These tools are the Wessex Head Injury Matrix (WHIM) and the JFK Coma Recovery Scale-Revised (CRS-R).

The Wessex Head Injury Matrix (WHIM) is a behavioural observation tool. It consists of 62 items in a roughly hierarchical order from least to most difficult, which provides a sequential framework of behaviour covering a patient's level of responsiveness and interaction with their environment. Behaviours observed and noted by the WHIM may occur either spontaneously or in response to sensory stimulation. The WHIM can monitor small changes from coma through to emergence from post-traumatic amnesia in patients with TBI (Shiel, Wilson, McLellan,

Horn, & Watson, 2000). Marjerus, Van Der Linden and Shiel (2000) also report its use with stroke patients. Returning to patients with TBI, another widely used assessment tool is the JFK Coma Recovery Scale-Revised (CRS-R). This consists of 25 items arranged hierarchically in six subscales: auditory, visual, motor, oro-motor (involving lips, tongue and jaw), communication and arousal. The scale is useful to make a differential diagnosis of VS, MCS and emergence from MCS. It measures responses in a standardised manner from reflexive to higher cognitive behaviours (Giacino, Kalmar, & Whyte 2004; Kalmar & Giacino, 2005).

On admission to the RMC, Gary's total score on the WHIM was 5, with the highest score recorded at number 14 (mechanical vocalisation such as a yawn or a sigh). His score recorded on the JFK CRS-R was 3. This is consistent with the vegetative state as described by Giacino and colleagues (2004) and illustrated in Table 7.1.

Gary was referred for a neuropsychological assessment as soon as he was admitted to the RMC and was first seen 2 days later in his bedroom at the RMC. He was in bed; his mother and other members of his

Table 7.1 Gary's Scores on the JFK Coma Recovery Scale-Revised

JFK CRS-R	Auditory Function Scale	Visual Function Scale	Motor Function Scale	Oro-motor/ Verbal Function Scale	Communi- cation Scale	Arousal Scale	Total Score
4 months post injury (On admission to RMC)	0	0	0	1	0	2	3
5 months post injury (Shunt re-adjustment)	1	1	2	1	0	2	7
9 months post injury	1	1	2	1	0	2	7
10 months post injury (cranioplasty)	1	1	2	1	0	2	7
12 months post injury	1	1	2	1	0	2	7
14 months post injury	1	1	2	2	0	2	8

LIVERPOOL JOHN MOORES UNIVERSITY
LEARNING SERVICES

family were present and provided some background information. There are sometimes disagreements between family members and professionals, as families may see behaviours not observed during formal assessment and/or may come to different interpretations of any behaviours observed. Nevertheless, it is important to listen to families, as they may be aware of emerging or purposeful behaviours that clinicians can miss. Gary was assessed with the WHIM (Shiel et al., 2000). For the first neuropsychological assessment, Gary was seen on nine occasions between February and May 2012. He was assessed in several different locations, at different times of the day and with different people present. The locations included his bedroom, physiotherapy and art therapy, and he was attended at different times by his mother, other members of his family, Mieko (art therapist), Birol and Zak (physiotherapists), Samira (occupational therapist) and others. Most observation sessions lasted between 20 and 30 minutes. Gary was usually awake and remained quiet, although sometimes he made a sound (a hiccough or an "oh" sound), and sometimes his left arm would shake. On the final occasion (May 2), he showed signs of distress when on the tilt table with his neck collar on; he made more noise and moved his head frequently. When the neck collar was removed, he calmed down.

The conclusions in May 2012 were as follows:

1. Scores indicate that Mr Hayward tends to be more responsive when he is on the tilt table although on one occasion he fell asleep while on this table.

2. His highest ranked behaviour on the WHIM is number 26 ('grimace to show dislike'). He did this when Samira, his OT, was using a swab to stimulate him with various tastes. When he tasted bitter, he made a definite grimace.

3. His mother reports that he shakes his arm to communicate. This may be true but may also be a reflex action.

4. His mother also says he is better when he is lying on his side and is also more responsive when he listens to his favourite piece of music. This was not observed but he was only seen once when lying on his right side and once when listening to music. His mother also reported that on one occasion Gary wept real tears. Again, this was not observed.

5. These results suggest that Mr Hayward was probably functioning in the vegetative state but may have been close to the minimally responsive range.

6. It is possible that the good response seen on May 2 could indicate a slight improvement but it might also be that he was being stimulated more that day.

7. There is debate as to whether or not Mr Hayward is to have a cranioplasty. If he does then he should be reassessed once he has recovered from the surgery. If not, then he should be reassessed in two to three months time to see if there is any change in his behaviour.

Barbara A. Wilson (consultant clinical neuropsychologist),
May 3, 2012

In August 2012, Gary had the cranioplasty, so in September 2012, he was referred for a further assessment to determine if there had been any change in his functioning. He was seen seven times in September and October. The WHIM was re-administered each time. He was observed mostly in physiotherapy, including one of his Padovan sessions, and on two occasions members of his family were present. As before, Gary was usually awake, occasionally making a sound, and sometimes his left arm shook. He appeared to be more alert since the cranioplasty, although his responsiveness varied. The conclusions at the time were:

1. Although Mr Hayward appeared to be more alert this time in that he did not fall asleep, there would not appear to be any real change in his functioning.

2. The average number of total behaviours over the test sessions earlier this year was 6.0. This time the average was just below 6.3, probably not a significant difference.

3. Mr Hayward's mother tries hard to get him to respond and it may well be that he is better with her, but this is hard to verify and document.

4. His mother is also worried about his shunt. The nurse manager was asked when the shunt was last inspected and reported that it had been checked in August 2012. Mrs Hayward, however, thinks that her son has the wrong shunt and she would like to have a second opinion on this.

5. In short, there appears to be no real change in Mr Hayward's condition. He seems to remain in a vegetative state.

Barbara A. Wilson (consultant clinical neuropsychologist),
October 4, 2012

When next seen in January 2013, there had been an obvious improvement in Gary's abilities. He responded clearly to Samira's requests such as "Lift your head" and "Take the clicker". When Samira telephoned his mother, Mr Hayward took the phone, held it to his ear and appeared to be listening. When his mother said goodbye, Mr Hayward handed the telephone back to Samira with no prompting. The report noted that he had made a clear improvement and was following commands. Thus he had emerged from the vegetative state and was now in the minimally conscious state.

Gary, like most patients at the RMC, attended art therapy. This has been practised as a psychological therapy since the 1940s and uses art media as its primary mode of communication. Art therapists encourage patients to express their feelings and emotions through art, such as painting, clay modelling and drawing (Barker & Brunk, 1991; Chapman et al., 2001). There are very few art therapy services in neurorehabilitation centres in the United Kingdom and even fewer which focus on the use of art therapy as a part of a physical rehabilitation programme. It is, however, an integral part of the rehabilitation programme at the RMC and is offered to most of the patients, including those who are in a minimally conscious state. Art therapy is believed to provide help for cognitive, emotional and physical problems.

Meiko Aida, the art therapist, first saw Gary in his room within a week of his admission. He was sitting in his wheelchair with his eyes slightly open and looking downwards. He did not make eye contact or move his head or eyes when spoken to. Meiko showed him some postcards, but he did not focus on them. She explained what Gary could do in art therapy, and again he did not respond. As Meiko felt that he would nevertheless benefit, Gary began attending art therapy twice a week on Saturdays and Sundays. The aim was to provide stimulations to develop alertness and to provide opportunities for passive movement in his hands and arms. There were three or four other patients attending at the same time. With hand-over-hand support (that is to say Meiko held Gary's hand over the paintbrush), together with narration of what was happening, he painted several watercolours. Meiko noted that on the May 13, 2012, Gary kept his eyes wide open, and looked at the therapist. When more alert he seemed to vocalise more by sighing and yawning. On June 16, he made a clear vocalisation ("Num num num. . .") during his art therapy session. At the end of July 2012, Gary painted his daughter's portrait from her photograph in his album, and by October 2012, he completed portraits of all his children from his photograph album. He also completed his self-portrait. All these were with full hand-over-hand support from Meiko.

Even though Gary was not working alone, he was being stimulated during his art therapy sessions. On October 14, while Gary was painting his portrait, he stuck out his tongue, so Meiko suggested he did this again, which he seemed to be attempting to do as his mouth opened slightly. He also lifted his left arm in response to a question from Meiko.

On November 11, 2012, Gary held the paintbrush by himself. He was encouraged to reply to questions by squeezing the therapist's hand or by putting his thumb up. On one occasion, at the beginning of December, Meiko asked him to stop moving the brush so as to change paint colour. He appeared to do so (this is the month Gary emerged from the VS into the MCS). The hand-over-hand support now stopped. Gary seemed to enjoy moving the brush by himself and smiled slightly. In the same month, December 2012, Gary began rolling and pinching clay. He made some clay beans and put them in the cup one by one. In January 2013, Gary picked up the paintbrush and held it by himself. He was also able to put it down gently. In February 2013, Gary started to lift his head upright when prompted. He waved to say goodbye when he left the room. He became assertive and would not let Meiko support his left hand, shaking it off. He made eye contact with and seemed to point to the material he wanted to use. At the beginning of March, he shook hands in greeting. In May 2013, when the other staff felt that he had emerged from the MCS, Gary looked at the work of another patient and nodded in recognition of his work. He also turned the pages of a book.

Thus, in art therapy, he seemed to be emerging from the MCS earlier than most of us observed and when the WHIM scores from Samira suggested he was still in a MCS. This is probably because Mieko was using a different cutoff point and not the one from the JFK CRS-R that Samira was following.

Another therapy offered at the RMC is oil dispersion bath (ODB). This was developed in Germany in the 1930s by Werner Junge as a special hydrotherapy technique (Büssing et al., 2008). Büssing et al. say:

> Based on the phenomenon that oil and water do not mix and on recommendations of Rudolf Steiner, Junge developed a vortex mechanism which churns water and essential oils into a fine mist. The oil-covered droplets empty into a tub, where the patient immerses for 15–30 minutes (p. 9).

For patients in vegetative state and minimal awareness, the ODB is recommended in order to stimulate and to harmonise proprioception and enable them to feel their whole body. The bath therapy given in this way is also stimulating an experience of being completely supported and nourished.

Gary began ODB, with oxalis oil, three weeks after admission. This was designed to address his hypersensitivity to touch when he responded by withdrawing his limbs and by making involuntary, rhythmic, muscular contractions and relaxations (clonus). His muscle tone fluctuated, and he was often in a completely flaccid (limp) state. The effect of the substance from the oxalis plant present in the oil seems to help the body release tension. Bath treatments for Gary continued with a combination of arnica oil with hypericum oil to further address the effects of physical trauma and persisting tachycardia (raised heart rate).

Six weeks after admission, cochlearia oil (an extract from horseradish root) was introduced. This oil is a strong stimulant. The aim was to see if Gary's alertness and responses would improve while he was treated with this substance.

Four months after admission, Gary's tachycardia persisted. The ODB then reverted to the use of arnica and hypericum oils. These combinations had a noticeable effect in bringing Gary's pulse rate to normal limits, whereas previously it had been erratic. It is possible that was simply due to the relaxing effects of a warm bath.

In addition to the ODB therapy, other anthroposophical treatments were administered during the early days. These included

1. Warm foot bath with sulphur bath lotion for ankle mobility
2. Oral care with calendula lotion and medicinal gargle
3. Skin care with body wash with citrus bath milk and calendula nappy change cream and balsamicum ointment for the perineal area

A further therapy Gary received whilst at the RMC was craniosacral therapy. This therapy was devised by Dr John Upledger in the 1979s. It is classed as an "alternative therapy" and involves light touches on the bones of the skull (including the face and mouth), spine and pelvis to release tension and improve body movement. To date there is little scientific evidence to support claims that craniosacral therapy helps in any specific disease. However, there is anecdotal evidence that it helps some people with an acquired brain injury feel more relaxed and offers some relief for symptoms of stress and tension.

Gary was admitted to the RMC 4 months after his trauma. He had not yet had his cranioplasty, and his cerebro-spinal fluid pressure was fluctuating. His shunt was adjusted several times during the first few weeks of his treatment period. Because of this, his craniosacral therapy was restricted, as no massage could be applied to part of his skull. Thus his cranium was monitored while the release of tension focussed on the upper thoracic, neck and occipital areas.

Gary was assessed by two speech and language therapists, Angela Hinchcliffe and Mandy McLeod. He was first seen by them in March 2012 (5 months post injury), when he was found to be making very little response to any auditory or visual stimuli. He showed no change in facial expression except in response to pain, and he produced an occasional voice but no intelligible words. A true assessment of his comprehension and expression was difficult to make due to his limited responses.

He was seen again by the speech and language therapists in June 2012 (8 months post injury) whilst standing upright on the tilt table in physiotherapy. The general impression was that he was slightly more responsive than when previously seen but that his communication skills remained severely limited. No voice was heard except in coughing, and he was unable to follow simple commands such as "close your eyes" or "open your mouth". He was tongue pumping and making reflexive swallowing to clear his own secretions. It was difficult to know whether Gary was able to focus on the speech and language therapists and, on occasion, appeared to be sleeping with his eyes open. A new communication goal was set at this time to try to investigate whether Gary could make any definite response to verbal input. If at least one reliable response could be established, then there would be a chance of developing a yes/no response system. This would afford Gary much more choice and enable us to evaluate his comprehension more accurately. Unfortunately, no such definite response was identified, and this goal was put on hold.

Gary was also seen for a pre-assessment for consideration of swallowing rehabilitation on June 22, 2012. He did not open his mouth apart from when yawning. His tongue was furred and white with oral secretions, resulting in drool. He showed minimal vocalisation and a withdrawal pattern or hypersensitivity to digital examination of his mouth. A plan was made to start baseline monitoring for evidence of any pre-swallowing skills. A chart needed to be drawn up and filled in to show any response to an oral stimulus (such as mouth care) in the form of a cough, swallow, increase of oral secretions, drooling, tongue pumping or vocalisation. Any other incidents of coughing, swallowing, drooling or vocalisation were also to be charted up. Evidence of clear responses of this kind would allow further assessment of swallowing.

In addition to the assessments and therapies described, Gary was receiving sensory stimulations three times a week. Sessions were conducted during different times of the day in different environments, including his own room, in the physiotherapy gym while standing on the tilt table, in the presence of his family and in the presence of his carers and other staff who regularly worked with him. To maximise possible movements from Gary, his splints were taken off during the sensory stimulations. Although he was demonstrating reflexive and spontaneous behaviours, no purposeful behaviours were noted during the first 14 months following the trauma.

Wilson and colleagues (2013), replicating and extending an earlier study by Elliott and associates (2005), demonstrated that, for patients in a state of reduced consciousness, there is a statistically significant difference between assessments carried out when patients are assessed while lying down, sitting in a wheelchair or upright on a tilt table or standing frame. Most patients showed more behaviours when in the upright position and fewest when lying down. This was particularly true for patients in the MCS. This study confirmed earlier findings suggesting that positional changes can have an effect on the level of arousal and awareness among patients in the VS and MCS. We suggest that when patients are medically stable, an upright position will help increase their level of alertness. Healthy people are more alert when standing compared to lying down; we do not, for example, fall asleep when standing up; this is likely to be true for patients with disorders of consciousness, too. The upright position could be built into therapy sessions. For example, feeding could commence when patients are on the tilt table at an angle of 45 degrees, with the angle being gradually increased. Grooming could also take place on the tilt table. This would also provide opportunities to benefit from auditory and visual input; spoken communication is easier to achieve when patients are upright; verbal prompts and hand-over-hand guidance to enhance tactile and proprioceptive feedback is easier when patients are not seen lying in bed. In physiotherapy, patients could initially begin standing on a tilt table at 45 degrees and then, depending on their tolerance, gradually progress to 90 degrees. Adopting this approach could enhance weight bearing and also help to prevent early onset of osteoporosis.

Gary was assessed in these three positions and, not surprisingly, showed more behaviours when upright. No significant changes were observed, however, in the total pattern of behaviours in relation to the lying and sitting positions. Thus he was like the VS patients in the Wilson and colleagues (2013) study.

Samira, Gary's occupational therapist, also observed that time of day affected Gary's behaviour. He tended to keep his eyes closed and be less responsive during the afternoon sessions. He was more responsive in the mornings and in the evenings. In addition, the left wrist movements were more prominent during morning sessions and when he was seated in his wheelchair.

Gary was unable to communicate verbally or non-verbally using any gestures or augmented aids. He was not following any visual and auditory instructions. Therefore all his care needed to be anticipated. A strict sensory stimulation and communication protocol was tailored in an attempt to meet Gary's needs (see Box 1).

Box 1: Protocol for sensory stimulation and communication with Gary

- Greeting Gary. Help Gary become oriented to person, place, time; e.g. tell Gary who you are (name and designation), where he is, what day and time it is during every session.
- Speak to Gary as if he understands what you are saying.
- Keep information simple and structured and use short sentences.
- Wait after every instruction to give Gary enough time to react or respond.
- Stand in front of him (eye level) while approaching him.
- Minimise the distractions, e.g. make sure only one person is talking at a time, close the door to avoid other interruptions, switch off the radio etc.
- Gary to be informed prior to each activity, e.g. It's time for your shower. This is the flannel. Hold the flannel in your left hand.
- Maintain privacy and dignity.

As Gary was more awake in the mornings and evenings, his sessions took place mostly during these times of the day. Also the sensory stimulations took place, for the most part, when he was in an upright position, as we had demonstrated he was more likely to be responsive and exhibit more behaviours then.

Gary's responses to visual stimulations were fluctuating between no responses to reflexive responses (for example blinking) to responses that were attempts to withdraw from a stimulus. On most assessments, no reactions were noticed in his left eye in response to light. His right eye showed minimal and inconsistent responses to visual threat. Gary was shown and asked to track photographs from his family album. He could not do this. This is summarised in Box 2.

Box 2: Gary's responses to visual stimuli

Responses	Stimuli
Right eye blink to light	Torch, family photos, therapist's finger
Right eye blink to threat	
Right pupil constricts to light	
No response with left eye	

To obtain more information on his poor vision, Gary was referred to an ophthalmologist, whose report 1 year post injury concluded that "Gary has good corneal sensitivity in both eyes and good blink reflex. He has a divergent left squint. He has good pupillary reaction in the right eye, but not in the left. He does have an indirect reaction in the left eye".

Gary's responses to auditory stimulation were no different from the visual stimulation. Once again his responses were noticed to be at the reflexive level. He was frowning, blinking his eyes, flexing his left elbow and/or repetitively moving his left wrist in a flexion-extension pattern: that is to say he was making a jerky movement with his wrist in response to loud auditory stimuli such as clapping and door banging. He did not respond when his name was called by familiar or unfamiliar people. During this period, Wendie and Zowey were often telephoned by Samira to see if Gary would respond to them. However, Gary did not show any reaction. He was reminded of memorable events which had happened to him in the past, but once again, he was unresponsive and did not show any changes in facial expression, nor did he make any gestures.

Gary was more sensitive when his face was touched compared to his limbs and other body parts. His reactions to facial touch varied from a startle reaction to closing his eyes and to frowning. On the other hand, when his limbs were touched, he showed a withdrawal response. Such reactions were obvious during grooming tasks such as when his face was washed with a flannel or when foam was put on prior to shaving and when his teeth were brushed. He resisted having his teeth brushed. Gary had developed tone and some movements in his left upper limb and, although he was not using these movements voluntarily, Samira tried to encourage these movements in a functional way in an attempt to overcome the reflexive movements and to use these movements more purposefully. Cleaning Gary's teeth or providing mouth hygiene was difficult for the rehabilitation assistants because of his hypersensitivity to touch around the face and mouth areas. Right from the beginning, Gary closed his mouth tightly when attempts were made to clean his teeth. This increased sensitivity could be the result of a lack of normal experience of sensation around and inside his mouth. Using hand-over-hand assistance, Samira used a vibratory toothbrush and shaving razor to maximise sensory stimulation.

The face, mouth and hands are rich in sensation; hence using sensory-motor learning and methods of facial oral tract therapy (FOTT; Coombes, 2008) which involves slow movements, facilitating hand-to-hand and hand-to-face contact, guided contact of his hands to face/mouth thera-peutically and during functional activities were administered. One of the FOTT principles – that is, skilful handling to influence posture, movement and sensation – was helpful in establishing good head and neck position-ing while encouraging Gary to open his mouth to allow mouth hygiene. Therapeutic techniques included jaw support and preparatory techniques such as a firm stroke with the therapist's fingers externally to his mouth and lips during pre-oral hygiene. Oral hygiene was used as an effective sensory stimulation of touch, texture, temperature and taste. Gary was also receiving these exercises during his Padovan therapy sessions. (More details of Padovan therapy, FOTT and neuro-functional re-organisation are provided in a later section in this chapter).

Gary's responses to olfactory and gustatory stimulations were, once more, reflexive in nature. Samira tried a number of olfactory stimula-tions from mild to strong flavours of essential oils (horseradish, lavender, eucalyptus, mustard seeds, ginger, olbas, fresh lime and coffee), scents and deodorants. Gary frequently used to pump his lips before swallow-ing. The swallow was often delayed. For gustatory sensations, the fol-lowing stimuli were used: peppermint mouthwash, swabs with water, lemon juice, apple juice, cranberry juice and coffee.

On admission, Gary had a flaccid tone with no voluntary or involun-tary movements in his upper or lower limbs. Gradually over a period of 5 months, his muscle tone started developing with the presence of involuntary movements in both upper and lower limbs. The muscle tone then increased in his left elbow extensors, his left knee flexors and his left ankle plantar flexors muscle groups, resulting in spontane-ous movements in both upper and lower limbs. He was observed to be flexing his right elbow and rapidly started moving his left wrist in a flexion-extension pattern with or without stimulation. As he did not have any head and neck control to maintain his head and neck in an appropriate alignment, Gary was provided with a cervical collar. About 10 months post injury, Gary was able to hold his neck upright for 10 to 12 seconds. In order to enhance the muscle strength in his head and neck, he was exercised on a floor mat in the prone position, that is to say lying on the floor propped up on his elbows. This occurred during combined sessions with occupational therapy and neuro-functional therapy (Padovan) sessions. The use of the cervical collar was gradually reduced.

At this stage, Gary was working on the tilt table and doing mat exercises in the physiotherapy gym four times a week. He was also seen daily by his physiotherapist for chest examinations. His sessions consisted of (1) passive range-of-motion and stretching exercises of both upper and lower limbs; (2) sitting balance; (3) postural correction; and (4) head-neck strengthening exercises. Because of increased tone in his left hamstring, he received Botox therapy 8 months post injury. Botox is a toxin used in cosmetic surgery to smooth out wrinkles but is also used in brain injury to relax tight muscles. After this, Gary was able to maintain an upright position on the tilt table for 30 minutes without distress to his breathing, blood pressure or other vital signs. About 10 months post injury, Gary started to use the standing frame alternated with the tilt table. As he was still struggling with low muscle tone, staff needed to be present all the time he was in the standing frame. They were asked to encourage or help him keep his head upright. Occasionally, Gary was able to raise his head and maintain this for 8 to 10 seconds without help. He also received sensory stimulation while on the standing frame. This position helped maintain stretching of the lower-limb muscle groups and also helped promote weight bearing.

Functional tasks were used to help increase Gary's muscle tone. For example, he was required to sit at the edge of his bed in order to carry out activities of daily living; or his neck muscle was gently stroked to help him lift his head up. While sitting, his right side was fully supported because of his flaccid tone. Thus his right elbow was extended to enable weight bearing. He was, however, able to keep his left elbow extended, as he had sufficient muscle tone on this side.

Gary was on medication for his epilepsy, which was well controlled. Nevertheless, he had two seizures, one 8 months and one 10 months post injury. His medication and his recovery patterns were regularly reviewed by the neuro-rehabilitation medical consultant. Gary also attended regular appointments at Kings College Hospital to monitor his shunt and to discuss his cranioplasty appointment. Five months after the assault, Gary had a CT scan, and the report stated,

There is an extensive cranial defect in keeping with the history of operation given. A large proportion of the left frontal and temporoparietal regions have been removed with a corresponding bone defect. There is a VP (*ventriculoperitoneal*) shunt in a satisfactory position. There is no evidence of significant hydrocephalus although there is still some midline shift with compression of the left sided ventricular system. This all represents post-surgical change and nothing is identified as potentially new.

Ten months post trauma, Gary's rehabilitation assistant noted a stone in Gary's incontinence pad. This was reported to the physician in charge, who referred Gary for an ultrasound of his urinary tract. The urinary report showed that

"the right kidney contains several hyperchoic foci, the largest is in the mid/lower pole and measures 8 mm, there is acoustic shadowing suggestive of a stone. In the upper pole there are several small stones/gravel. No hydronephrosis or focal lesion was seen. The left kidney is sonographically normal with no stones demonstrated. Good cortical thickness and vascularity seen bilaterally. The bladder is thin walled and normal in contour".

For a time, Gary was on and off antibiotics for urinary tract infections. In December 2012, he had an operation (laser cystolitholapaxy) to break up and remove the bladder stones.

Regular formal review meetings involving members of Gary's family were held to discuss Gary's complex care and treatment needs. These included medical, nursing and therapeutic needs. Every 4 to 6 weeks, Gary's condition was discussed with his family. Samira coordinated these meetings. Practical information and emotional support were provided to the family. The local commissioners who were funding Gary's treatment at the RMC were also updated with Gary's progress. As Gary was still in a vegetative state and not in a position to participate in formal goal-oriented rehabilitation, staff and family members who were tasked with Gary's best interests formulated his treatment goals. The goals were:

- Management of Gary's physical disability, including monitoring his muscle tone and posture, managing his spasticity and preventing contractures and pressure sores
- Enteral feed management (feeding directly into the stomach through his PEG tube)

- Infection control and management
- Appropriate stimulation and ongoing assessment of behavioural responses
- Family support

Almost 15 months post injury and 5 months after the cranioplasty operation, Gary emerged from the vegetative state into the minimally conscious state. For the first time, he followed a command, "Hold your head up". Although he only did this once, the response was appropriate to the context. One month after this single episode, more behaviours were observed when he was being assessed with the WHIM. These were "Making eye contact", "Increased arousal and agitation prior to urination and defecation", "Looking at the person giving him attention", "Tracking a source of sound", "Performing physical movement on verbal request" and "Imitating gestures with his left hand". At this stage, Samira formulated goals to try to make these responses more consistent. As Gary was showing a withdrawal reaction to tactile stimuli, a goal was formulated to reduce withdrawal and teach him to localise responses using functional objects. The goal was worded as: *"Gary will consistently use his left hand to localise stimuli, such as his shaving brush, to enhance his self-awareness and awareness of the environment".*

Soon Gary started showing more purposeful and less reflexive responses to olfactory and gustatory stimulations. He began moving his left hand towards olfactory and gustatory stimulations. This was followed by rapid movements in his left wrist in the flexion-extension pattern together with frowning and grimacing. Once he made a fist and then a claw with the fingers of his left hand while showing clear anger on his face in response to the olfactory stimulus of mustard oil.

At this stage, Samira attempted to develop a more consistent pattern to the olfactory and gustatory stimulations. Two goals were formulated as:

1. Measure the difference in Gary's responses between familiar (cologne and perfume) and un-familiar (mustard oil) or neutral (water) olfactory stimuli
2. To increase our understanding of Gary's likes, dislikes and interests by observing how Gary expresses preferences towards familiar and unfamiliar gustatory stimuli using water, fizzy drinks and salt

As Gary had active movements in his left hand, Samira planned to use these movements in functional tasks: for example, using the flannel to wipe his mouth. This goal was formulated as: *"With verbal prompting*

Gary is to use his left hand to wipe his mouth or to wipe dribbling saliva using a paper towel".

Once Gary started achieving these goals, more demanding goals were set. At this stage, he still had very limited visual functioning, although his other senses, especially tactile and auditory, were working well. A clicker was chosen as a stimulus to work with because of Gary's tendency to move his left hand in a flexion/extension pattern. Thus, he was taught to use the clickers. Later, these were used as a communication aid. Soon Gary started using the clickers appropriately. He clicked when he was asked to click and stopped when he was asked to stop. Later on, he was taught to click once for "yes" and twice for "no". Once he had mastered the clickers, the task became more demanding by using a buzzer for "yes" and "no". To make the task more familiar and meaningful, Samira recorded John (Gary's father) saying "yes" and "no" so that when Gary pressed the buzzer for "yes" or for "no" he heard his father's voice saying the appropriate word.

To maintain upright posture of head and neck, Gary was frequently reminded to lift his head up using verbal and physical prompts. Physical prompts were in the form of a gentle touch with the therapist's index finger to encourage him to raise his head. These prompts were gradually faded out. Sometimes Gary showed some agitation and tried to move Samira's finger away from his chin.

Together with attempts to improve his cognition and communication, Samira started to work on Gary's upper-limb mobility, including both fine and gross movement patterns. This was accomplished with dumbbell exercises, transferring marbles to a container and catching and throwing a ball. Gary was encouraged to lift a half-kilogram dumbbell 10 times to allow elbow flexion and extension so as to strengthen his muscles. Initially, he was provided hand-over-hand assistance, which was gradually reduced. The task was made more difficult to see whether Gary could count from 1 to 10 on his own and stop the activity after ten repetitions without verbal or physical prompting. Although Gary was not counting the numbers loudly, he appeared to be aware of this simple calculation as he followed the instruction correctly. Furthermore, Gary was able to follow the same instructions when transferring marbles. Here, he was asked to transfer a particular number of marbles from one bowl to another and was successful. His tactile senses were good. His left-hand fine motor skills were improving, and he was able to use his left hand in several functional tasks such as wiping his mouth. His dominant right hand, however, was not so good. To improve functioning in his right hand, Samira planned to engage him in a bilateral therapeutic task such as catching and throwing a ball. Despite his very poor vision consequent to his brain injury, Gary could locate the ball with his left hand. At first he only located it; he did not throw or catch it. He seemed to be using his hearing to determine where the therapist was, then he felt for her hand in order to give the ball to her.

By now, Gary was giving consistent responses to Samira with the clickers (press once for "yes" and twice for "no") and then to the buzzers (producing "yes" and "no" sounds). Consequently, the demands were increased, and Gary was required to answer a series of questions generated by Wendie and Samira. Ten questions were produced (see Box 3).

Box 3: Yes/no questions generated for Gary to answer

Questions	Correct answer
Is your name Gary?	Yes
Were you born in March?	No
Do you have children?	Yes
Is your mum called Wendie?	Yes
Are you Mr Nicholson?	No
Is your son called Martyn?	No
Did you used to run a pub?	Yes
Is your sister called Zowey?	Yes
Is your mum's dog's name Tom?	No
Are you a doctor?	No

In January and February 2013, 14 and 15 months post injury, Gary was reviewed by Mandy, one of the speech and language therapists. Her impression was Gary had a severe oro-pharyngeal dysphagia consistent with overall presentation of a low awareness state. She recommended FOTT (Coombes, 2008) should continue in order to facilitate Gary's control of his tongue and tongue movements. This provides a comprehensive approach to the assessment and treatment of disturbances in facial expression, oral movement, swallowing, breathing, voice and speech conditions caused by neurological conditions. It covers four main areas: nutrition, oral hygiene, non-verbal communication and speech movements.

The stages of the FOTT exercises to be given before oral hygiene commences are:

1. The therapist uses hand-over-hand guidance to provide face stimulation (this seems to be better tolerated by the patient).
2. The therapist strokes his/her finger on the patient's face (in four quadrants: right and left upper and lower jaw) in preparation for entering the mouth (next stage).
3. The therapist, using a wet finger, rubs the gum from the back to the front. This step is repeated for the four quadrants right and left of the upper jaw and the same for the lower jaw before moving on to the lips.
4. The final stage is for the patient to brush his or her teeth, with the therapist providing hand-to-hand guidance.

The hand-to-hand guide to touch the face was indeed better tolerated by Gary. It was double stimulation (hand and face), as he was touching his face with his own hands. This was done before Lorena, the Padovan therapist, approached his face for the exercises. After this, the therapist gave a firm touch (a stroke) with a finger externally to the mouth (to prepare Gary for the next stage, entering the mouth). The inside of the mouth was then stimulated with a rubbing or brushing movement on the gum from back to front. This was repeated on the other side and then on the lower jaw. The jaw was supported during the stimulation technique. All these exercises also helped improve and/or facilitate swallowing.

Since January 25, 2013, Gary had been given sips of water to see if he could manage this; next, well-diluted cranberry juice was tried in a beaker with a spout. He was helped to extend his elbow. When given the beaker, he attempted to lift it but would not drink. He also declined a teaspoon of ice cream offered to him. Mandy recommended the following:

1. To continue with FOTT
2. Sips of plain water only or well-diluted squash via an open cup or spouted beaker. Only Wendie or Lorena, the Padovan specialist, to do this.

At the same time, Gary was receiving regular mobility exercises from his physiotherapist 5 days each week and a combined neuro-functional therapy (Padovan, 1992) and occupational therapy sessions twice a week. This helped maintain the integrity of his joints and improve the muscle strength in his upper and lower limbs. During the physiotherapy sessions,

Gary worked on rolling, transfers (getting from one place to another) and sitting balance exercises. In addition to stretching and exercises involving range of motion, he was upright in the standing frame and using the thera-trainer equipment. This is a static exercise bicycle which enables patients with a disability to restore movements. Other benefits include improving circulation, maintaining muscle power, improving flexibility, stimulating metabolic processes, improving bladder and bowel functions and decreasing fluid retention.

Slight improvements were noticed in his mobility levels at 16 months post injury. With the assistance of two staff and using a modified pivot transfer (meaning the person can bear at least some weight on one or both legs and spins to move his or her bottom from one surface to another), Gary began learning transfer techniques. He was using his left hand to help. The effort he put into this, at that time, was estimated to be about 10%.

Gary was able to sit unsupported if his right elbow was stabilised into extension. However, he had a tendency to push towards the right side with his left hand. He was able to sit with his feet supported on the floor for 10 seconds using his abdominal muscles, his left hip flexors and his left hand to reach for the bed. When in the standing frame, he needed less external support to maintain an erect posture. He was able to actively extend his neck both with and without a verbal request and physical assistance. He was able to hold his head upright for 5 to 10 seconds without support while in the standing frame or when sitting on the edge of a plinth. When he was helped to move from the sitting to lying position by two assistants, he was using his left leg and arm independently with some verbal prompts. He had regular positioning as well as a splinting regime for his ankle and for the left knee joint. He tolerated these well. After the Botox administration, there was a 10% increase in the passive range of his left hip extension. Other joint ranges were maintained.

He was coping well with the range-of-motion and stretching exercises for his lower limbs and was, in general, participating in these. However, on some occasions he resisted the exercises and pushed the therapist's hand away. He also did this on occasion during his Padovan therapy. He started to resist movements which required him to use his left arm during rhythmical exercises, especially on his left lower limb, probably because this was painful.

From the time of his admission to the RMC, while he was still in a VS, Gary received neuro-functional re-organisation (NFR) sessions from the Padovan method twice a week. Each session lasted between 45 and 60 minutes, with two or three members of staff assisting. NFR is a rhythmic, synchronised exercise regime that encourages the link between neurological organisation and developmental progress. With Gary, the NFR focussed on exercising all four limbs, his head, neck, trunk and mouth. Influenced by the idea that the processes of walking, talking and thinking are interconnected and dependent on one another but nevertheless manifested at different stages in a child's development, the physical exercises involved in NFR follow a sequence that resembles the walking process, starting from a horizontal position and gradually going through the activities of rolling, creeping and crawling, to reach the vertical position. The sequence was adapted according to Gary's abilities and needs. More exercises were added to the sequence while Gary was regaining consciousness (or awareness) and muscle strength, allowing him to perform some of the exercises actively by himself or with minimal support if required. He began in the supine position (lying face up) on the plinth in physiotherapy, then progressed to the prone position (lying face down) before advancing to the mat on the floor to enable rolling, creeping and crawling. As hands have a large cortical representation, it is important to exercise these, too, again using a neuroevolutionary approach. Initially Gary's hands were moved passively until he was able to move his hands by himself and copy or follow the therapist's hand movements.

In NFR, exercises are accompanied by verses from songs sung by the therapist. Not only does this provide rhythm to the movement, it also provides auditory stimulation by making associations, allowing exposure to a broader vocabulary than general conversation, encouraging imagination and stimulating memory and thinking. The singing can also emphasise the purpose of the various movements and encourage motivation. Wendie was involved in choosing songs for Gary. As he loved the band Queen, for some movements, the therapists sang "We Will Rock You" from Queen. In addition, other verses were specific to the movement patterns worked on. These combined auditory and tactile stimulation. Thus, one song was about pedalling and sung to Gary while he was working on pedalling movements.

One surprising finding was that, as Gary started to wake up, he demonstrated that he remembered and knew the words of the verses sung to him while he was in a low awareness state. As soon as his voice began to return, he joined in with humming the rhythm of the verses. In fact, he appeared to be trying to say the right words, even though he was not always correct due to his language impairment, which prevented him from articulating and finding the right words.

The Padovan method has two parts: the sequence described earlier, which is comprised of physical exercises, and the oral motricity or mouth exercises. The latter focuses on the vegetative reflex functions

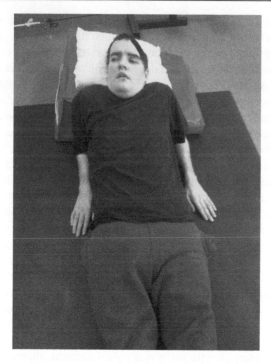

Figure 7.1 Gary in physiotherapy soon after admission to the Raphael Medical Centre

of respiration, suction, chewing and swallowing. When Gary was in a VS, stimulation of the face and mouth was performed using vibration and a spatula. Breathing exercises involved blowing a whistle to pass air through Gary's mouth and/or nose. As he began to regain consciousness, he was reluctant to have these oral motricity exercises and refused some of them. He started to show aggression towards the therapists by hitting or kicking out at them. This kind of behaviour is not uncommon and can be seen as a typical phase as patients emerge from the VS or the MCS and become more aware. We asked Wendie to observe his behaviour in his NFR sessions and to intervene when necessary. One of the principles in the Padovan method is that the role of parents, relatives or friends is fundamental, as it eases a patient's anxiety and frustration. It was also important for Wendie to see that Gary's recovery was progressing. Wendie's presence seemed to calm her son. Once his difficult behaviour reduced, Gary started to participate more during the sessions and began to progress and slowly improve, as we will see in Chapters 9, 10 and 11.

Chapter 8

Cranioplasty
Surgical repair of a skull deformity

Gary had a cranioplasty in August 2012. A brief account of the history and details of this operation are provided.

Historical perspective

It is important when considering cranioplasty that we are aware of the evolution of such a procedure. Cranioplasty has a long history, and historical records suggest that Incan surgeons performed trepanation on infants that were epileptic (Kakar, Nagaria, & Kirkpatrick, 2009). Trepanation has its origins in the Greek word "trypanon", which means to "bore", and this is akin to the procedure we now know as decompressive craniectomy. Historical evidence suggests that following trepanation, the Incan surgeons then performed a cranioplasty using precious metals. While evidence of procedures which we now call "craniectomy" and "cranioplasty" date back to 4000 BC, it was not until the 16th century that the term "cranioplasty" was mentioned in literature, when the use of a gold plate was referred to by the physician Fallopius. Then in 1668, Job Janszoon van Meekeren, a Dutch surgeon, is recorded to have used canine bone to repair a cranial defect in a Russian man. In the late 19th century, we start to see recordings of surgeons and physicians attempting bone grafting, and in the early 20th century, the use of auto grafts (using the patient's own tissue) for cranioplasties became the treatment of choice. It was during the 20th century, particularly after World War II, there was a large need for cranioplasty, as increased warfare led to head traumas resulting in surgeons needing to look for alternatives to bone grafting. At this time, methyl methacrylate (an acrylic resin) started to be employed in cranioplasty. There is continuous debate about the best substance to be employed. Throughout history, many different materials and techniques have been described, but today there is still no consensus about the best material. Research continues looking at both biologic, that is, improving the ability of the host to regenerate bone, and using non-biologic substitutions such as metals and plastics, with the aim of developing the ideal reconstruction materials (Aydin et al., 2011).

Decompressive craniectomy

The decompressive craniectomy is often seen as a potentially life-saving procedure in the management of patients who have a medically intractable intracranial hypertension secondary to severe traumatic head injuries or following significant strokes (Aaribi et al., 2006). More recently, this procedure has also been used following subarachnoid haemorrhage, intracranial infection and inflammatory conditions (Ahmed et al., 2010; Baussart et al., 2006; Güresir et al., 2009). During the procedure, the surgeon temporarily removes a large segment of the skull in order to provide extra space into which the injured or oedematous brain can expand. This can be performed either unilaterally or bilaterally depending on the severity of the injury or swelling. This technique was first described by Harvey Cushing in 1905, and decompressive cranioectomies have been increasingly performed since that time even though the efficacy of such a procedure is still highly controversial. There is also similar controversy around the necessity of cranial reconstruction, a cranioplasty after such a procedure (Yang et al., 2003).

Decompressive craniectomy is often an emergency procedure performed in an effort to reduce intracranial hypertension. Following the procedure, patients often commence their rehabilitation pathway together with the resulting skull deficit. A cranioplasty has often been recognised as being required for two main reasons – protecting the brain exposed through the skull defect and for cosmetic purposes – both of which, in the rehabilitative process, have significance. However, more recently, there has been an increasing body of evidence which proposes that cranioplasty may have an important part to play in the acceleration and recovery of patients' neurological status. To date, the reason this procedure should positively impact neurological improvement remains essentially unknown.

Pickard and colleagues (2005) note that the natural history after head injury is for patients to improve, and if they do not, we should ask why this is so. They go on to say that those patients who have a large skull defect because of a craniectomy may go on to develop "the syndrome of the trephined", otherwise known as "sinking skin flap syndrome". Pickard and colleagues (2005) say this is more likely to happen if the patient is dehydrated and is seated upright for prolonged periods.

"Sinking flap syndrome" is essentially an unusual syndrome in which neurological deterioration occurs following removal of a large skull bone flap (Joseph & Reilly, 2009). This syndrome is usually character-ised by dizziness, headaches, neuropsychiatric features, language prob-lem fatigue and motor deficits (Stiver, Wintermark, & Manley, 2008). There is little understanding about the primary pathology of this syn-drome. There have been a number of hypotheses, including the effect of atmospheric pressure over the bone (Flint et al., 2008); changes in cerebrospinal fluid (Fodstad et al., 1984); issues with venous drainage, changes in blood flow and metabolic aetiology (Erdogan et al., 2003; Isago et al., 2004; Kuo et al., 2004). It is possible that all these play a part in the observed neurological deterioration noted in removal of a large skull bone flap.

Many case studies and clinical series suggest that early cranioplasty may prevent delayed complications of decompressive craniectomy such as the aforementioned sinking flap syndrome.

Does cranioplasty improve functioning?

Improvement in neurological status and cognition

There have been several studies reported in the empirical literature which suggest that following cranioplasty, there are noted improvements in neu-rological deficits, cognitive function and brain haemodynamic (Chieregato, 2006; Isago et al., 2004; Kemmling et al., 2010). Such reports purport that there are potential benefits to patients to undergo a craniotomy procedure, as positive changes to cognition might follow. It would appear in the lit-erature that it is becoming increasingly apparent that varying elements of neurological improvement are more common than previously thought.

Agner and associates (2002) reported improvement in cognition fol-lowing cranioplasty using the Cognistat measure. This is a neurobehav-ioural cognitive status examination which assesses different aspects of language, performing complex constructions, memory, calculations and reasoning. They also used the EXIT interview, which assesses executive, functioning at the bedside. In both these measures they report 48.3% and 32.9% improvement, respectively, between pre cranioplasty and after cranioplasty in a single case study.

In another case study, Maeshima and colleagues (2005) reported cognitive improvement on a number of neuropsychological measures (Word Fluency Test, Frontal Lobe Assessment Battery, Auditory Ver-bal Learning Test, Raven's Coloured Progressive Matrices and Revised

WAIS, MMSE, and the Behavioural Inattention Test) following cranioplasty. The results on these measures also correlated with the data of the patient's cerebral perfusion.

Honeybul and colleagues (2013) conducted a prospective cohort study whose findings noted a measurable improvement in an aspect of neurological function in 16% of the patients ($n = 25$) who underwent a cranioplasty. Outcome was based on assessments completed a few days prior to and after the procedure. Di Stefano and colleagues (2012) reported a series of case studies in which they noted a deterioration of motor and neuropsychological deficits prior to the patients' cranioplasty and a subsequent unexpected improvement in performance on a neuropsychological battery and a series of motor function tests immediately after cranioplasty. This was also seen in the work reported by Bender and associates (2013), who identified 147 patients who had cognitive and motor deficits prior to cranioplasty and were assessed following the procedure. Their findings highlighted that patients with shorter delays to cranioplasty (< 86 days) had a better functional outcome than patients with longer delays of > 85 days.

When one considers that decompressive craniectomy is often performed as an emergency procedure in order to stop further damage to an already damaged brain, then we need to consider how this affects future rehabilitation.

It is well recognised that rehabilitation has been shown to improve neurological outcome by improving physical, cognitive, emotional and behavioural deficits commonly seen after acquired brain injuries. Rehabilitation is about enabling and empowering an individual to achieve appropriate independence through meaningful activities of daily living and social integration (Gordon et al., 2006; Sorbo et al., 2004). However, given rehabilitation facilities and services are scarce resources, it has been argued that they should be provided appropriately. When considering the impact decompressive craniectomy can have on neurological recovery there has been a suggestion that intensive neurorehabilitation should be delayed until a cranioplasty has been performed (Jelcic et al., 2013). However, should this be the defining factor by which a patient receives or does not receive neurorehabilitation, given that these patients will not be provided with the benefit of early rehabilitation? Because cranioplasties are frequently not performed until after 12 months post injury, it could be argued that these patients might never reach their full potential. Di Stefano and colleagues (2012, 827), as a result of their study, conclude that noted neuropsychological and motor improvements following cranioplasty should "serve as a reminder to

rehabilitation clinicians to give serious consideration to prompt performance of cranioplasty during the time allotted for the rehabilitation of
these patients". Such findings highlight the issue of optimal timing of
cranioplasty.

Timing of cranioplasty

Readings in the literature suggest there might be an optimal timing for
performing cranioplasty both for neurological outcome and for any
complications that may occur. It was originally thought that having a
short time, less than 3 months, between decompressive craniectomy and
cranioplasty, led to poor outcome thus leading to varying periods of
time between the two procedures (Kumar et al., 2004). More recently,
though, this has been challenged, with an increasing number of studies
suggesting that cranioplasty can be performed sooner with safe outcome
and that the procedure should not be intentionally delayed. Neurological
opinion highlights the fact that when considering the ideal timing, the
issues that should be considered are residual brain oedema, brain retrac-
tion into the cranial vault, risk of infection and delayed post-traumatic
hydrocephalus (Di Stefano et al., 2012).

When considering optimal timing, Rish and colleagues (1979) reported
that the highest complication rates were noted when cranioplasties were
performed 1 to 6 months following decompressive craniectomy, whereas
those performed 12 to 18 months after decompressive craniectomy,
showed a significantly lower rate of complication. One of the main reasons for delaying cranioplasty was the issue of infection risk, given the
surgeon would be intervening in a contaminated wound, such wounds
being noted in large open skull fractures or penetrating head injuries
(Foster et al., 2002). Later research concurs with the findings reported
by Rish and associates and in particular with the clinical series reported
by Schuss and colleagues (2012) and Thavarajah and associates (2012).
Both these clinical series suggest the lower complication rate is due to
the lowered risk and possibility of surgical wound contamination, given
the cranioplasty was delayed.

Tasiou and colleagues (2014) in their systematic review emphasise
that the reported complications noted in early cranioplasties might be
due to the decompressive craniectomy and issues with the index head
injury rather than with the performed cranioplasty. Other studies concur with this thought and suggest that complications noted in early cranioplasty are due to bone dislocation, reporting that anatomic location
was more important in considering the procedure rather than timing for

the development of procedure related infections (De Bonis et al., 2012). There would appear that in recent literature, authors believe that there is a definitive advantage of early cranioplasty (approximately 2 months following the decompressive craniectomy). This, it is argued, is the optimal time rather than a delayed procedure. However, it has been highlighted that rather than adhering to a chronological 2 months, it is imperative the decision to perform the cranioplasty should be based on the neurological status of the patient, the progression of the neurology of the patient, infection on the scalp and in the wound, sinking flap and hydrocephalus.

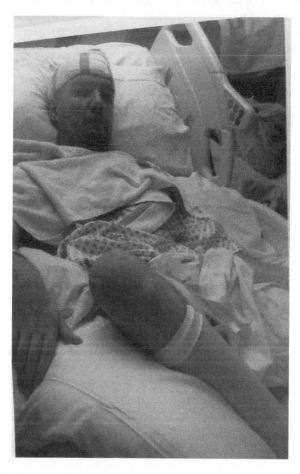

Figure 8.1 Gary, just after the cranioplasty operation

Overall, it has to be noted that cranioplasty is a relatively simple procedure. However, evidence indicates there is a high variability of complications following. It could be argued that to date there is an inaccurate estimation of complication rate and improvement rate. The majority of the existing studies are retrospective, and therefore findings are limited. When considering the issue of early cranioplasty and the optimal timing, there appears to be a lack of well-designed research studies: whilst there are a number of studies that highlight the need for early cranioplasty citing positive neurological, cognitive and motor changes, there are equal numbers of studies that cite that early cranioplasty is fraught with complications and that it is better to wait. However, there are significant findings across research which demonstrate that early cranioplasty minimises the risk of trephination syndrome (sinking flap syndrome), thus contributing to better outcome and overall prognosis in some individuals.

Gary and cranioplasty

Because of the decompressive craniectomy carried out soon after the assault, Gary underwent a cranioplasty 10 months following his severe head injury. Prior to the procedure, Gary had significant cognitive and motor deficits and was deemed to be in a vegetative state. Approximately 1 month following the cranioplasty, neuropsychological and motor assessments indicated no change, and he remained in a vegetative state. However, within 3 months of the procedure, he was following basic commands, and reassessment indicated he was no longer in a vegetative state and had emerged into a minimally conscious state. Considering the research already cited in this chapter, it would appear that while arguably Gary's cranioplasty was not within an "optimal time", that is within 2 months or less than 86 days, the procedure contributed to a better outcome and overall prognosis.

Chapter 9

Waking up

Recovery from brain injury is a long-term process. For Gary, it took more than 18 months to completely wake up. It was good to see improvement in Gary's cognition day by day; however, at the same time, Gary started having behaviour problems. These are often seen in patients who survive a traumatic brain injury once they regain consciousness, and they can be difficult to manage. This was true with Gary, and this behaviour was putting his life and recovery at risk. Being not only Gary's occupational therapist but also his rehabilitation co-ordinator, Samira was the focal point of complaints and concerns raised by the staff caring for Gary. Observations by the rehabilitation assistants and the family provided Samira with a global picture of his functioning, his current level of insight and his awareness of his limitations. Needless to say here is that Gary's level of insight was impaired, and consequently his safety was of major concern to all those involved in his care. He kept staff on their toes, for example, by trying to climb over the bed rails to get out of bed. In his best interests and using the least restrictive options, he was provided with an extra bed rail extension covered in foam padding to prevent him from falling and getting injured. A crash mattress was also placed on the floor next to his bed for additional safety. His bed was at the lowest height to further minimise the impact of trauma if he fell out of bed. The nurses were having a hard time positioning Gary in bed using the protocols provided by Samira. This was due to the fact that he started to throw pillows, positioning packs and other equipment out of the bed. The night staff also reported that he removed the tube connected to his feeding pump, and it was found lying on the floor. Gary was not only reluctant to do his exercises but refused to engage in his daily care activities, too. He began to resist movements during his Padovan sessions and showed his anger by banging his left arm on the mat or on his wheelchair armrest. He was making a fist and was resisting movements by holding the therapist's hand with his left arm. During personal care, especially during mouth care and shaving, Gary was again difficult and resisted the staff's attempts to carry out these activities. It was at this time, when he was distressed, that Gary uttered his first word post injury. This was an inappropriate word that Gary seemed to be using to indicate his unwillingness to participate in therapy.

Not everything was a problem, however. Improvements in mobility were a positive sign of recovery. Gary was distributing his weight by repositioning himself without help. Cognitive improvements were also noticed. His comprehension increased, and he showed signs of understanding and following simple auditory instructions. He started responding to closed-ended questions using gestures such as nodding and shaking his head to indicate "yes" and "no". At this stage, Gary stopped using the yes-and-no buzzer and, instead, he was encouraged to use gestures. He started to greet staff. Thus, if Samira said, "Hello Gary. I am Samira, your OT" and put her hand out where he could see it, he shook her hand. Although his vision was still poor, he was able to see shadows and could identify colours from the corner of his right eye.

He used gestures to express basic emotions such as pain, discomfort, mood and anger. At this time, he was reliably responding to yes-and-no questions through nodding or shaking his head. He was able to complete almost all items on the behavioural measures (the Wessex Head Injury Matrix and the JFK Coma Recovery Scale-Revised), so these were discontinued.

Physically, Gary was getting stronger. This was especially true of his left upper limb, but he was making active movements in his right upper limb, too, most noticeably in his elbow, wrist and finger joints. He tended to protect his right arm and was reluctant to use his right hand in functional tasks. He started to hold his head up for more than 5 minutes without prompting. He was receiving less support to maintain an erect position while on the standing frame. He was able to change his position in bed. He was rolling independently to the right using his stronger side; however, he still needed the help of one person to turn to his left side. The movements he could do himself needed to be incorporated into functional tasks in order to increase his independence. This was an essential step at this stage of his recovery. At this time, Samira was working alongside the rehabilitation assistants to ensure that Gary was participating in activities of daily living. Activity analysis protocols and goals with detailed action plans were tailored as required to meet his needs (see Box 4 and Box 5 for examples). The rehabilitation assistant played a vital role here by following these protocols and encouraging Gary to pursue the steps. Positive reinforcement in the form of praise, reassurance and feedback helped motivate him and continue the activity participation.

Box 4: Gary will be able to brush his teeth holding the toothbrush in his left hand with moderate assistance within 3 weeks

Action Plan	
1	**Facilitation of brushing task** during ADL session by OT; to be **carried over** by the rehabilitation assistant on other days.
2	Encourage him to **sit upright with his head up.** Place mirror in front of him and provide verbal and visual input.
3	Initially provide **hand-over-hand assistance** throughout the task and gradually wean off the support once task is achieved.
4	Ask him to rinse his toothbrush in the plastic cup, this to be followed with Gary encouraged to hold his toothbrush in his right hand and put the toothpaste on the brush with his left hand.
5	**Prompt and encourage** Gary to follow the instructions throughout. Keep instructions *short and simple*. Make sure they are loud enough.
6	Provide **positive feedback** on accomplishment of every successful single task, which will motivate him to engage more into therapeutic and functional activities.
7	**Strengthening exercises** for right and left upper limb including grip strength by the occupational therapist and the physiotherapist during one-to-one sessions.
8	Encourage him to use his right hand (dominant hand – pre accident) functionally while he is carrying out activities of daily living.
9	**Core strengthening exercises** to better tolerate sitting for longer duration by PT.
10	**Sitting balance and reaching exercises** to facilitate independent forward leaning position and independent use of right and left arm. To be carried out by the PT & OT.
11	**Record** all observations onto the inter-disciplinary notes.

In order to provide an objectively quantifiable measure of any deficits, Samira used the Functional Independence Measure (FIM; Granger et al., 1986) and the Functional Assessment Measure (FAM; Hall et al., 1993) to measure Gary's activities of daily living (ADL). As the WHIM and JFK CRS-R were discontinued due to the fact that he was at ceiling on these tests, the Putney Auditory Comprehension Screening Test (PACST; Beaumont et al., 2002) was used to measure his basic comprehension, and a range of motion and muscle tests were used to measure his motor ability. The test results, together with information from interviews with Gary, his family and the rehabilitation assistant, facilitated the generation of a problem list. A treatment plan, incorporating short-term and long-term goals, was formulated. Gary and his best interests were always the main focus. The long-term goal was for Gary to live and stay with his family. To achieve this, a list of short-term goals, including independence in activities of daily living, vision improvement and the ability to walk again, were determined. Although he still had a long way to go, Gary had come through the stage of a prolonged disorder of consciousness. This was to the surprise of many people who had not expected him to do so well.

On the standardised assessments, the FIM and the FAM, Gary's score was at level 1, which meant he required total assistance. Nevertheless, he was contributing a little to the activities. His contribution was assessed as being less than 25%, but he had only just emerged from the minimally conscious state, so this was felt to be reasonable. The effort he was putting in, even though negligible, was still valuable. At this time, Gary was receiving most of his nutrition through a PEG feed, but, at this stage, he began to take some liquid nutrition orally. He was provided with some devices to help him, including a mug with a lid to allow him to take in just small portions of liquid at a time. He was encouraged to hold the mug in his hand while drinking different flavoured juices, smoothies and a yoghurt drink. At first, Gary made faces and frowned after the first sip of the drink; however, he soon began managing drinks on his own. He was receiving supervision throughout these sessions for his safety. After a month, Gary was able to manage fluids from glasses and was by now safer and taking only small, careful sips. When being fed by the PEG tube, Gary began to help the staff by holding the PEG tube syringe upright while the nurses poured in the liquid.

The dietician came to review Gary's progress and determine a feeding regime. Gary started to take in food orally. He had a soft meal at lunchtime and some chocolate mousse either in the morning or evening. He was continuing to receive nourishment through the PEG tube. His medications were regularly reviewed by the neurorehabilitation consultant. His antiepileptic medication was gradually reduced. Botox was given again in his right calf muscle groups, as the muscle tone here was increasing.

Around 20 months post trauma, the speech and language therapist once again reviewed Gary's ability to swallow. His family was present at this time. Gary had improved since the previous assessment. He had been rated as having a severe oral-pharyngeal dysphagia (an inability to swallow). This was now changed to a rating of a mild to moderate oro-pharyngeal dysphagia (swallowing disorder). His swallowing ability was complicated by fatigue levels, distractibility and language impairments, which slowed down his progression towards a full oral diet and fluids. Occasional reminders were required for Gary to allow more time between sips of his drink and thus to decrease risk of aspiration (food entering his lungs) or laryngeal penetration (food entering the windpipe). He was improving in his lip seal (ability to close his lips) and had only minimal spillage with fluids. Sometimes he was able to drink and eat without any residue or spillage from his lips. He was naturally placing his head in a forward flexed position during swallowing. This was encouraged. Gary was supervised at all times while eating and drinking and, when fatigued, he was assisted.

His non-verbal communication had improved considerably, and he was able to localise to requests such as "look at me". He was able to attend to tasks for 1 to 3 minutes if he was in a quiet and noise-free environment. He was spontaneously nodding his head for "yes", although he required encouragement to shake his head for "no". If the content was too complex or if there were distractions in the environment, his yes or no responses were less accurate.

Samira once again interviewed family members to discuss their concerns and any goals they wished to work on for Gary, who, at this time, was unable to take part in the goal-setting process. Wendie was heavily involved in determining and guiding the treatment programme and helped evaluate Gary's impairment in activities of daily living such as eating, showering, grooming and dressing. She also advised on leisure activities such as listening to music. Samira assessed Gary's physical, cognitive and behavioural impairments which were affecting his various ADLs. An activity analysis of each task was performed and was used to guide the rehabilitation process. An example of the activity analysis for showering can be seen in Box 5.

Box 5: Activity analysis for Gary's showering

Shower protocol

Key points

- Prior to showering, please always ensure staff are comfortable and confident in carrying out the task, that vital signs have been taken, and Gary is medically stable. If during the session,

Gary's vital signs drastically change, immediately terminate the session removing Gary from the situation, call for help, and return Gary to bed.

- Please ensure Gary is never left alone, as Gary has a history of seizures. If he has an epileptic seizure, call for help and perform first aid.
- At the beginning of the session, please ensure that all the area is clear to assist with a safe transfer and that all equipment required (i.e. shampoo, towels etc.) are prepared so that, at no point, will you need to leave Gary to get anything.
- Please follow the step-by-step guide below on how to support Gary in the shower, and promote as much independence as possible. Please follow as closely as you can, making your own clinical judgements as to whether Gary is able to perform as suggested at that moment in time.

Before the shower takes place

- **Inform:** Inform Gary that it is time for his shower, and ask if this is ok.
- **Transfer: REQUIRES 2 PEOPLE FOR DURATION OF ACTIVITY.** Transfer Gary from bed to shower commode as set out in Physio transfer protocol.
- **Positioning:**

  o   Ensure the pelvis is touching the back of the commode.
  o   Ensure hips are aligned, facing forwards and at 90°.
  o   Use the hips as a guide to align knees, and feet, ensuring feet are on the foot plates at 90°.
  o   Use the hips as a guide to ensure shoulders and head are also aligned.
  o   Apply the safety belt, ensuring that the belt is not too tight/too loose by checking that you can slide two fingers breadth between Gary's pelvis and the seatbelt.
  o   Once the belt and harness are secure and you are sure that Gary is positioned safely and correctly, use the tilt mechanism at the back of the shower commode to tilt him back 30°.

There is limited space in the bathroom, so please take your time, and ensure the floor is dry at all times.

Once in the shower

Step 1: Turn on the shower and ask Gary to gesture when the water is at a good temperature for him.

(When washing his hair: guide Gary to wet his hair, put the shampoo in his LEFT hand, and guide him to wash the right side of his head, transferring to the left side and then rinse).

Step 2: Switch on the shower and prompt Gary to hold the shower head, and assist/guide him to wet his torso and upper arms with the shower. *Please note to switch off the shower when it is not being used*.

Step 3: Provide Gary with a flannel and ask him to wash his face.

Step 4: Provide a soapy flannel and prompt Gary to wash the right side of his neck.

Step 5: Prompt Gary to wash the right arm, starting from the shoulder and working down to the elbow. Then from elbow to fingertips.

Step 6: Prompt/assist Gary to wash the right side of his torso starting from the armpit and working down to the hip.

Step 7: Guide/assist Gary to wash the top of the right leg, starting at the hip and working down to the knee.

Step 8: Key worker to wash right lower leg, and assist rinsing of the body.

Step 9: **Repeat steps 4–8 prompting/assisting Gary to use his right hand as much as possible to wash the LEFT side of himself with key worker assisting where required.**

Step 10: Encourage Gary to use his left hand to wash the groin area. Assist where necessary.

Step 11: Guide Gary to rinse off all soap with the shower, and turn off shower.

To dry, please follow the same pattern.

At this time, Gary was still receiving total assistance for his grooming. Although his participation in grooming tasks was limited, his resistance to brushing his teeth had decreased. He was still reluctant to brush his teeth on his own, even with prompting, but he was opening his mouth with verbal prompting and was allowing his key worker to brush his teeth. He would also gargle and spit out water after his teeth were brushed. He needed verbal prompting to spit out the water or else he swallowed it.

By now, and with constant verbal and physical prompting, Gary was holding the flannel in his left hand to wash his chest and private areas.

When dressing, he required physical assistance to put his right arm in the sleeve hole of his T-shirt due to weakness in his right hand and his tendency to guard or protect his right arm. However, when verbally prompted, he took the garment over his head and put his left hand in the T-shirt arm hole by himself. Then he pulled his T-shirt down and adjusted it appropriately. He needed physical assistance to adjust his T-shirt from the back. His increasing ability to move in bed was utilised in dressing, and Gary was able to help change his pads and manage the dressing of his lower body by lifting his pelvis to help in the dressing process. Toilet training was also taking place to promote bladder and bowel continence.

Regular physiotherapy sessions continued so as to increase Gary's mobility and muscle strengthening. To relearn sequential developmental patterns, he had mat exercises during the combined neuro-functional therapy and occupational therapy sessions. Gary was receiving mat exercises in the prone position. Due to recent changes in his behaviour, he refused to do certain exercises even though he was prompted and given explanations from the therapists and, at times, from his mother, Wendie, as to why these were important. The exercises that he was prepared to actively participate in were mostly limited to rolling. These he could do with moderate to minimal assistance. With verbal prompting, he was able to roll from prone to supine (rolling on his left side) and from supine to prone (rolling on right side). Half rolling from supine towards his right side he was able to do independently. With assistance, he was maintaining elbow-propped prone lying positioning. His right shoulder and elbow had some weakness and required some support at times. Oral motrocity exercises were on hold, as he was strongly refusing any stimulation on his face and in his mouth.

Papiya, Gary's physiotherapist at the time, started seeing Gary for hydrotherapy sessions in addition to chest physiotherapy and gym sessions. In the gym sessions, he was rolling, practising transfers (for example, getting from his wheelchair to the bed) and sitting balance exercises. He was still using the standing frame and the exercise bicycle as well as receiving regular positioning and the splinting regime for his ankles and the left knee joint. He was tolerating the splinting well. He was able to roll independently to his right side and needed moderate assistance from one person to roll to the left. He was able to transfer between surfaces using a modified pivot transfer, with the assistance of two people. When changing from sitting to lying, he needed the help of two people, but he was using his left leg and arm independently and only occasionally needing prompts. During transfers, he used his left hand to hold on to a staff member who was assisting. In weight bearing, he was probably putting in 10% effort. In sitting he still had a tendency to push towards his right side with his left hand but, with prompting, he could maintain a stable position. Gary was able to sit with his feet supported on the floor for 10 to 15 seconds and used his abdominal muscles and his left hand to reach for the bed. When standing in the standing frame, he was supported with positioning aids to maintain an erect posture, but no supports were required to support his trunk laterally. He needed aids to facilitate a neutral ankle position and was able to actively extend his neck and hold this position for at least 5 minutes.

He was generally tolerating physiotherapy sessions well, but on some occasions he was resisting and pushing the therapist's hand away. On April 28, 2013, Botox was administered for the tight muscles on his right-hand side. This, together with a footbath, enabled him to receive intensive standing frame exercises.

Further neuropsychological tests were administered to monitor Gary's cognitive recovery. In November 2013, Gary was assessed with the Middlesex Elderly Assessment of Mental State (MEAMS; Golding, 1989). This is a screening test for major impairment of cognitive skills in elderly people, and Gary, of course, was really too young for this test. However, the MEAMS includes some simple tasks covering a range of cognitive functions and can give some indication of strengths and weaknesses for people emerging from the MCS. A test to detect visual impairments, the Cortical Vision Screening Test (CORVIST; Warrington, Plant, & James, 2001), was attempted but abandoned, as Gary had such limited vision. His eye operation was still 7 months away. On the MEAMS, Gary passed the three simple mental arithmetic questions and was able to follow a simple rule without errors ("When I tap once, you tap twice and when I tap twice, you tap once"). He failed orientation questions (such as knowing the year, the month and the name of the Raphael Medical Centre); naming parts of a watch, which he could feel (he named the watch itself but not the strap or the buckle); naming to description; verbal fluency; and learning a person's name. Subtests requiring him to see were omitted. On some informal tests of vision, Gary was unable to see objects, shapes or letters. He could see movement and could recognise most colours if he held an object close to his right eye. He could write his name, but his poor vision meant some of the letters overlapped.

The conclusions to the November 2013 report were:

1.   There is little doubt that Mr Hayward has improved considerably since his previous assessment in January 2013.

2. He is now too good for the Wessex Head Injury Matrix.
3. He was able to do simple mental arithmetic and follow a simple rule from the MEAMS.
4. He has word finding and fluency problems among other cognitive difficulties.
5. His vision is very poor.
6. Further recovery is likely. His mother works hard and is very supportive. Samira Dhamapurkar is also working well with Mr Hayward. With their help and support I feel Mr Hayward may continue to improve for a long time.
7. I am happy to reassess him in a few months time.

Barbara A. Wilson (consultant clinical
neuropsychologist), November 21, 2013

In June 2014, after the eye operation, which was a great success, Gary passed 8 of the 12 subtests of the MEAMS. The four failures were on orientation, naming (the watch strap and the buckle), unusual views (recognising photographs of objects taken from an atypical angle) and learning a person's name. In August 2014, he was 100% successful on all parts of the CORVIST! He was also given some tests of unilateral neglect and passed all with ease. By now, he was ready to be tested on more traditional neuropsychological tests, and in October and November 2014, he was seen several times for 45 minutes each time and given a range of tests. Gary was always willing to participate in the tests. He tended to give up easily when he found things difficult, saying "Oh I don't know, I can't do that", but he continued with the assessment nevertheless. He was always seen in his wheelchair. He remembered his timetable, where he had just been, where he was supposed to be next and when he last saw the neuropsychologist. His everyday memory appeared to be reasonable. His behaviour was always appropriate.

On the Visual Object and Space Perception Battery (VOSP; Warrington & James, 1991), Gary passed all the items administered, suggesting his visual perceptual and visual spatial skills were unimpaired. Not surprisingly, he struggled with some of the tests, particularly the verbal ones. He was just below average on a reading test (Wendie had said that she thought he was a bit dyslexic when he was at school). His memory, as measured by the Rivermead Behavioural Memory Test-3 (RBMT-3; Wilson et al., 2008) was patchy. He was average on some of the nonverbal tests (apart from face recognition) and tests of prospective memory (remembering to do things) but impaired at some of the verbal tests such as remembering a story and the orientation questions: although oriented in time and place, he failed to recall the names of the present and previous prime ministers and presidents of the United States). On one of the subtests from the Wechsler Adult Intelligence Test–4 (Wechsler, 2008), the Block Design Subtest, Gary scored above average, including getting extra points for being quick. As his neuropsychologist, I was surprised and jokingly said, "Gary, you haven't read the rule book, you are not supposed to do as well as this". He replied "Well, it's easy isn't it?" Needless to say, most people with severe brain injury do not find this subtest easy.

The conclusions to the neuropsychological report dated November 2014 were as follows:

> Mr Hayward has made a remarkable improvement since January 2013 when the Wessex Head Injury Matrix was last administered. This is a test for people with disorders of consciousness. Mr Hayward had been in a low awareness state for over 18 months. He can now be assessed with more traditional neuropsychological tests.

1. The Test of Premorbid Functioning suggests that Mr Hayward was probably functioning at the bottom end of the average range prior to his accident although this could be an underestimate as he scores above average on some nonverbal tests.
2. His vision is now good: he scored 100% on the Cortical Vision Screening Test.
3. He also has good basic perceptual and visual spatial skills as he passed easily all subtests of the Visual Object and Space Perception Battery and tests of unilateral neglect. In addition, Mr Hayward was above average on the block design subtest from the Wechsler Adult Intelligence Scale–4. Indeed his perceptual reasoning index on the Wechsler is perfectly normal.
4. He has some problems with verbal abilities: his verbal comprehension index on the Wechsler Adult Intelligence Scale–4 was at the third percentile; he had problems with prose recall and verbal fluency and he tended to do worse on the verbal subtests of the Rivermead Behavioural Memory Test–3. This is a reflection of the fact that he has left orbital-tempero-parietal damage while the right hemisphere is relatively undamaged.
5. He shows some executive problems, for example, he made several perseverations on the fluency tests and found it difficult to inhibit responses on the Hayling Test. Despite this, Mr Hayward did a little better on the more demanding switching tasks.

6. Mr Hayward's memory functioning is patchy. He does poorly on orientation (mostly because he does not know the names of the Prime Minister and the President of the USA) and on name learning, but his scores are reasonable on some of the nonverbal subtests such as route learning and also on prospective memory tasks. He remembers well what has been happening earlier in the day and what he is supposed to be doing next.

7. Not surprisingly, Mr Hayward is slow at processing information. His poorest index on the Wechsler was with processing speed. He also did not do well on the Trail Making tests. He did not make errors but was just slow.

8. Given that Mr Hayward still seems to be improving week by week, I would expect further improvement in his cognitive functioning to occur.

When Wendie was told that Gary's memory seemed pretty good, she said, *"What I've always said is when Gary woke up the first time, Gary had everything there. Now when he fell out the bed they guaranteed me more or less that no damage had been done to his brain. The brain had just shut down through shock. So if that was the case, he should still remember everything that he had remembered when he first woke up"*.

Art therapy report

During the summer of 2013, Gary became more alert and responsive. By June 2013, he was talking to the therapists and was able to answer questions verbally. He would not let Meiko support his right hand, preferring, instead, to use his own left hand to support his right hand. He did, however, watch while Meiko painted a "superhero" for him. He would not engage in any artwork himself at this time. His verbal skills increased throughout July and August. He became more motivated to engage with art therapy, spontaneously holding the paintbrush, writing his name, looking at a book of wild animals, turning the pages himself and drawing an elephant. He also wrote some letters with coloured pencils. In general, he was more relaxed during the session and joined in singing a song with the other patients and the therapist.

In September, he once again refused to engage in the therapy or singing. This was shortly before his eye operation. On October 13, 2013, Gary attended art therapy for the first time since the operation. He wanted his carer to stay with him. He was talkative when he was introduced to other group members, saying, "I don't know her". He was given a lump of clay and was able to roll it with some help. His carer made a duck. Gary felt this and said, "I can't see". He also said, "What's the point of doing this?" But nevertheless he made a human form. On November 10, Gary came to the art room with his carer; he arrived early and the room was still full with the previous group members. He refused to stay. Following this, art therapy was discontinued at Gary's request.

Chapter 10

Rehabilitation through music therapy (with a contribution from Melanie Cornell, music therapist)

Gary had always liked music, particularly by the group Queen. Since he was admitted to the Raphael Medical Centre (RMC), he had regular music therapy.

Music therapy is a psychological intervention and an established health profession in which music is used as the main tool of communication. Clients are engaged in a therapeutic relationship through musical interaction to help them with physical, emotional, cognitive and social needs. After the assessment of a client, music therapists create a bespoke treatment programme of improvised and pre-composed music, using a combination of instrumental music and voice, either sung or spoken. The ability to respond to music appears to be innate. Music therapists use the emotional qualities and rhythmical, melodic and tonal components of music to provide a process through which clients can be supported to communicate, express their feelings and rehabilitate without the need for musical skill or a musical background (Magee, 2005).

Melanie, the music therapist, first saw Gary on March 2, 2012, for a music therapy assessment approximately three weeks after his admission to the RMC, when he was still in bed. She saw him again a few days later, on March 8, to follow up the assessment. This time, Gary was seen in the music therapy room in his wheelchair. Melanie wrote her first report soon after this. She noted that Gary showed few signs of response to music. He was asleep for most of the first session and was heard to snore. His left eye was sometimes partly open and his right eye shut. Ten minutes from the end of the second assessment, however, Gary opened his left eye wider and was able to keep this open for the rest of the session. When familiar music was played, he sporadically opened his eyes wider, and he occasionally appeared to look in the direction of the musical stimuli. He sometimes yawned during musical stimuli and moved his lips with a chewing motion. He produced some slight vocal sounds, which sounded like hiccoughs.

Gary began receiving individual music therapy from March 2012 for 30 minutes, once a week. During the sessions, Melanie played familiar songs both live and recorded. She also provided hand-over-hand facilitation to explore accessible instruments such as the drum, guitar and wind chimes. In Melanie's second report, in May 2012, she noted that Gary appeared to be fatigued at the beginning of the sessions, but when familiar songs were played, particularly those by Queen, he seemed to be more alert, as his eyes widened, he made some sounds and his left hand began to shake. Melanie believed that Gary was more responsive to guitar playing and singing than to other instruments.

By the third report in June 2012, Melanie noted that recently Gary appeared to be awake throughout most of the 30-minute session. He moved his left eye more often. Sometimes this appeared to be in response to her singing a familiar song or when she played the guitar or the drum. Occasionally Gary seemed to look in the direction of the music, but it was difficult to be certain of this. His eyes were open wider; he yawned, sighed and pumped his lips during familiar songs. He made some vocalisations which were sometimes in the same pitch as the music. Occasionally, Gary showed some changes in facial expression such as slight frowns or the beginnings of a smile during songs by Queen or Frank Sinatra. Again, it was difficult to be certain of this.

Nine months after starting music therapy, in December 2012, Gary showed signs of increased alertness. When familiar songs were played, he opened his eyes for longer periods, pumped his lips and vocalised a little. Gary's left arm often started shaking at this stage of his recovery. When this happened, Melanie placed a djembe drum in front of him so he could experience drum playing. He was provided with other opportunities for sensory experiences by feeling the vibration of the guitar. Melanie placed Gary's hand on the guitar while she was playing and noticed that when this happened, Gary seemed to be more alert. Melanie also saw changes in Gary's facial expression when familiar songs were played.

After a year, Gary became increasingly alert, and this may have been due to a general improvement as a result of several different therapies over time. He was able to stay awake longer. He often made eye contact when Melanie spoke to him and responded to questions by shaking his head. Sometimes, when Melanie offered Gary the guitar or drum, he pushed her hand away. Another behaviour noticed by Melanie was that Gary often kept his head lowered until she sang songs to him while playing the guitar, at which point he would raise his head and look in the direction of the instrument. He then began to be sleepy again during sessions.

In January 2013, it was decided that Gary might benefit from a break from music therapy for 3 months. This was partly because of the time pressure of other therapies, partly because he had begun to push Melanie's hand away when she placed a musical instrument next to him and partly because he was sleepy during the sessions. He recommenced music therapy in April 2013.

In July 2013, Gary began to respond verbally to questions with yes and no and greet the therapist with "hello". He continued to improve and was, of course, by now well out of the minimally conscious state. Melanie noted that Gary's alertness and ability to interact continued to increase. In the early sessions, he would often sleep. He had made fantastic progress in his levels of alertness and ability to engage.

In her report dated September 5, 2013, Melanie wrote,

> "Gary is responding very well, in particular to songs by his favourite group Queen, he immediately starts nodding his head to the music and singing the words throughout the songs. He also responds by holding his head up and looking at the music therapist. He has started to smile and laugh during singing and during interaction. He is responding with his hands moving to the rhythm and melody of the music. When Melanie Cornell played one of his favourite songs Gary moved his hands to the music, laughed and began singing with the music therapist. He appeared to relax and calm down during singing. Perhaps this took his mind off any possible discomfort he was feeling. It is clear that he enjoys singing and interacting through music. He is also participating in conversation about the songs. Again, these reactions are indicative of a general improvement over time resulting from natural progress; the advances resulting from several therapies he has been receiving; as well as the enhancements to his reactions to music, one of his favourite pastimes".

In August 2013, Gary began singing songs with Melanie. He nodded his head to the music, sang the lyrics, held his head up and made eye contact. He also began to smile and laugh while singing and interacting with Melanie. In addition, he began moving his hands to the music. At this point in his music therapy, Gary held the guitar and explored it with his fingers for the first time. Previously, he had always pushed it away when it was offered to him. He tried moving his left hand on the fret board as if trying to play chords and attempted to pick the strings using this hand. He needed support in reaching his right hand to the strings. Initially, he seemed apprehensive and said he could not feel the strings with his right hand. With guidance, however, he started to move his fingers on the strings. He was willing to record his music and laughed when he heard it back; it seemed to boost confidence in his abilities.

Gary was also willing to make music on the iPad using the Smart Keyboard and the Smart Guitar. He was required to touch the screen to play the virtual guitar and keyboard. He said he enjoyed this. He was also able to make choices about which instruments he wanted to play. At times, he appeared to perseverate on tapping the instrument, although this seemed to last only for a few moments. He enjoyed hearing back the recording of his playing. He expressed surprise that it was himself playing, and this seemed to increase his confidence. He appeared calmer and brighter in mood and showed greater willingness to engage in his music therapy sessions and actively participate in music making. Melanie showed Gary a photograph she took of him playing guitar at a previous session (see page 84). Gary looked at it closely, smiled and laughed, seemingly proud of his achievement.

By November 2013, Gary was increasingly aware of his situation, and his motivation to attend or engage in the music therapy sessions appeared to be affected by his mood or level of agitation. Sometimes he refused to attend and became more agitated if encouraged. Nevertheless, on average, he attended two out of four sessions a month. When he did attend, he was able to engage in the session and showed interest in listening to familiar songs, particularly by Queen and Frank Sinatra. As soon as the music started, Gary moved to the music, nodding his head, looking up at Melanie and singing all the words. He started to imitate the melody of the instrumentals by whistling or humming. He moved his hands to the music. He was able to state the name of his favourite band, discuss the band and name the singer. As he had word-finding problems, he sometimes found it hard to express himself, which led to frustration. However, as soon as the music started, he began to sing, which seemed to help him relax and build up his confidence.

By April 2014, Gary was once again attending regularly. He engaged more confidently in musical and verbal interaction throughout the session. He was more spontaneous in his play and often began singing spontaneously. He knew all the words to familiar songs, particularly those by Queen. He often chose to sing rather than play. Sometimes he was reluctant and had low confidence in his ability to play instruments. In June 2014, he had an operation to restore his vision. Then he started to play the drum and the tambourine without being prompted. He began using both hands in his play more frequently. He showed particularly good fine motor control and co-ordination when playing along to a well-known beat to the song "We Will Rock You". He often expressed enjoyment of singing and more recently of playing. He was more confident in trying a wider range of instruments including the piano, drum, tambourine, guitar and virtual instruments on the iPad. This seemed to coincide with his restored vision.

In general, Gary appeared happier in the sessions and more fluent in verbal interaction. Although he occasionally became frustrated when unable to find the word he was looking for, the agitation was no longer as intense as it once had been. His memory for song lyrics and melodies was amazing. He was able to sing entire songs and play guitar and drum solos, which he acted out with his hands as he sang the tune. He also remembered details of the music therapy sessions.

As a result of continuing advances in all aspects of his rehabilitation, Gary seemed to extend his enjoyment in singing. He was able to sing a range of songs, including singing the melody to guitar solos. He could mime the drum solos by tapping his hands on his knees while he sang the lyrics. He was able to remember previous sessions, freely express his thoughts and share memories and feelings triggered by songs. Around this time, Gary had his eye operation, which meant he could see again. After he regained his sight, he remained motivated to play the guitar and was willing to relearn chords with Melanie.

Melanie summarised Gary's journey through music therapy. She said he continued to be more spontaneous in his playing and singing. He often began singing spontaneously and could sing all the words to familiar songs. After regaining his sight in June 2014, he showed more interest and motivation in playing percussion instruments. In his first session after the operation, he spontaneously asked to play the guitar. He held it appropriately and used both hands freely to strum and play notes on the fret board. He showed much-improved co-ordination and fine motor control of both hands.

Gary continued to be brighter in mood and more fluent in verbal interaction. The agitation noticed soon after he 'woke up' rarely occurred by the summer of 2014 and, when it did, Gary was able to manage it calmly. He continued to freely express his thoughts and feelings and memories triggered by the music. As stated before, he had an amazing memory for song lyrics and melodies.

Table 10.1 Gary's Progression Through Music Therapy

	Admission	After 9 months	After 12 months	After 16 months	After 17 months	After 28 months	After 32 months
Eye opening	✓						
Pumping lips		✓					
Slight vocal sounds		✓					
Left hand shaking		✓					
Signs of smiles		✓					
Shaking of head			✓				
Lifting head			✓				
Pushing away with hand			✓				
Verbal communication			✓				
Nod head to music				✓			
Mouthing words				✓			
Smiling				✓			
Laughing				✓			
Shaking of left leg				✓			
Singing lyrics to songs					✓		
Playing guitar					✓		
Music making on iPad					✓		
Sharing memories triggered by songs						✓	
Writing a song							✓

Figure 10.1 Gary in a music therapy session

In November 2014, Gary said he wanted to write his own song about his rehabilitation journey. The themes he expressed he would like to write about were how he felt before the accident, how he felt coming out of his coma and how he feels now and looking to the future. He is currently working on this while continuing to sing songs and play instruments during his music therapy sessions. On New Year's Eve 2014, he went to a concert featuring Queen with some friends. This took some arranging by Wendie, and it cost her quite a bit of money, but he made it. He went there and back in a taxi with his brother-in-law and said it was great.

Gary's first session back with Melanie was on February 26, 2015. His progress can also be seen in Table 10.1

Chapter 11

Ongoing rehabilitation

Gary was receiving intensive rehabilitation, with treatment sessions focused on increasing his independence in self-care and functional mobility, so he had to be able to transfer independently. The physiotherapists administered passive ranges of motion with prolonged stretching to maintain joint integrity and to prevent soft tissue contractures. Resistive exercises using weighted cuffs, dumbbells and the multigym, for example, were performed within the available range of motion. Adaptive equipment, such as a plate guard for easier self-feeding and shirts that could be pulled over his head rather than buttoned, were provided to help Gary be more independent. Around 20 months post injury, an occupational therapy assessment showed that Gary required the help of another person for all areas of personal self-care and functional mobility. It took another 2 months before Gary started to show progress in many self-care areas such as eating, swallowing, grooming, bathing and dressing his upper body. Because of the increased range of motion and better muscle strength in his upper limbs, together with improved cognition, Gary was now able to participate in his self-care to a greater extent.

Samira assessed Gary in his room while performing his morning self-care. He needed maximum assistance when transferring from his bed to a wheelchair or onto a commode. He was able to dress, groom and feed himself with assistance from the rehabilitation assistant. The main problem areas identified included right-sided weakness, decreased functional mobility (that is, transfer skills), impaired vision and decreased basic self-care. The short-term goals, those to be achieved within 2 to 3 weeks, were (1) being able to wash with moderate assistance and maximum verbal prompting and (2) being able to brush his teeth during oral care with moderate assistance. The long-term goals, those to be achieved before discharge, included: (1) being able to perform all grooming tasks while seated at the sink with supervision; (2) being able to pull on an overhead T-shirt under supervision; (3) being able to perform functional transfers such as move from his bed to his wheelchair or shower chair with contact guard assistance or transfer board; and (4) being able to take a shower with distant supervision. Someone needed to be present for safety reasons, as Gary might have had a seizure. Treatment sessions focussed on all areas of basic daily care in order to achieve maximal independence so that Gary could reach the long-term goal of discharge home.

Gary was by now eating soft meals and was managing his meals in a reasonable period of time. He needed supervision and physical assistance while he was eating because of his limited vision. Thus his key worker scooped the meal on to a spoon and gave this to Gary, who could then eat with his left hand. He started drinking by himself without any assistance. Later, and despite the fact that a plate guard was provided to increase independence, Gary became frustrated when he was unable to scoop the food. He refused to eat and threw the spoon away. The occupational therapists then used a "backward chaining" procedure to teach Gary to eat. In backward chaining, the person learning is prompted or guided through a complete task, say putting on a coat, then guided through all steps of the chain except for the last one, which he or she is required to complete without help; then the last two steps of the chain are omitted and so forth. Forward chaining is also used, in which case the first step of the chain is the first to be omitted instead of the last. Backward chaining is usually preferred and more likely to be used in rehabilitation, probably because it is always followed by positive reinforcement and is easier to administer. So in Gary's case, through the use of backward chaining, the therapist or the assistant helped with most of the task, and Gary was asked to do the last step of the sequence. Completion of the task was positively rewarding for him. Then Gary was asked to complete the last two steps and so on. He was receiving daily repetitive practise during his activities-of-daily living sessions. Practice continued with Gary completing further steps once he was successful with the earlier steps. As Gary had low tolerance for frustration, the backward chaining method always guaranteed some success and seemed a good teaching method for him. A protocol (see Box 6) was drawn up for Gary's eating programme.

Box 6: Backward chaining progress chart for Gary's eating programme

Goal: For Gary to eat his lunch with the supervision of one member of staff with assistance in 3 weeks' time.

Step No.	Step Description	Level of assistance
1	Gary to be comfortably positioned in his wheelchair and with the therapist or the rehabilitation assistant next to him.	Total
2	With assistance and using the appropriate adaptive aids (such as the plate guard to prevent food from spilling) help Gary to pick up the spoon. Provide hand-over-hand assistance.	Total
3	Inform Gary what he is going to eat. (This is essential, as Gary has limited vision).	Verbal prompt
4	Ask Gary to hold the spoon with his left hand.	Verbal prompt
5	Use hand-over-hand technique to guide Gary to scoop the food out of his bowl or plate.	Verbal and Physical prompt
6	Use reduced assistance to help stabilise his hand to bring the spoon up to his mouth.	Verbal and Physical prompt
7	Stop assisting and use a verbal prompt to ask Gary to put the spoon in his mouth.	Verbal prompt
8	Prompt Gary to take spoon out of his mouth and swallow.	Verbal prompt
9	Repeat the process.	

Improvements were also noticed in his grooming tasks. Gary started washing his face, holding the flannel in his left hand. He was still reluctant to brush his teeth, wash his hands and shave. He opened his mouth with verbal prompting and allowed staff to brush his teeth. He still required verbal prompting to gargle and spit water after brushing. Poor insight made it difficult for Gary to spit, so he was still swallowing the water. His participation in many functional tasks was not perfect due to his very limited vision, his restricted mobility and the fact that he continued to protect his right arm. In the shower, his participation was limited to washing his chest, abdomen, right arm and thighs using the flannel in his left hand. He was receiving maximum assistance and putting less than 50% effort into completing the washing tasks.

Gary's dressing skills improved, and he progressed from needing maximum assistance to moderate assistance with his upper-body dressing. However, his limited vision and mobility in his lower limbs and his tendency to protect his right arm hindered his independence in dressing. When putting on his T-shirt, once he was assisted with his right arm, he was able to pull it through the neck and could thread his left arm into the right hole. He was also beginning to adjust his T-shirt from the front with some help from a member of staff. He needed help to retrieve his clothes from the drawer. With regard to dressing his lower half, he was only able to raise one side and lift his pelvis. He needed total assistance for toileting and maintaining perineal hygiene. Gary had no control at this stage of his bladder and bowels.

Improvements in his cognition and speech were also observed. He was more aware of his surroundings. Significant gains were made in his verbal expression and responsiveness to verbal directions. In addition, he was more willing to go to speech and language therapy sessions and to use his voice, which previously he had been reluctant to do. He began to say "yes" and "no" to questions and to express some basic emotions in words such as "angry" or "happy" although he still needed verbal prompts to do this. He could now count from 1 to 20 and sing the alphabet from "A" to "Z". Furthermore, he could sing a few verses of his favourite song, "We Will Rock You" by Queen. Although Gary was still disoriented in time and place, he could now recall the names of some family members. At times he perseverated in his speech, frequently saying "oh man", "yeah" and "no". Therapy sessions had focussed on combining the ease of output with modelling and encouragement to use his voice while playing songs from his CDs in his room. A song was played, and when the chorus came on, the music was paused, and he was encouraged to fill in the words when the music was re-started. He was then able to voice and sing the chorus to approximately 80% of the songs played. He tapped his hand in time to the rhythm, too. The name of the song was then written down in large lettering on a white board and, by the second stanza of the chorus, he continued to sing the chorus with encouragement and with increased clarity of voicing. He enjoyed this task, and it was felt important to facilitate such verbalisations. There was a photograph album of family members in Gary's room at the RMC. He could name approximately 90% of them accurately. The few failures were thought to be due to his poor vision and lack of picture clarity rather than a language impairment. Some writing practise had commenced. Gary, however, was reluctant to write and to hold the marker with hand-over-hand assistance. Occasionally he was scribbling on paper when asked to make a straight line or any geometrical figure or the alphabet. Figure 11.1 shows Gary in his room, with a clear view of his cranioplasty scar.

LIVERPOOL JOHN MOORES UNIVERSITY
LEARNING SERVICES

Figure 11.1 Gary and his cranioplasty scar

During this period of rapid recovery, Gary's behaviour passed through a number of different stages. As mentioned earlier, angry outbursts and behaviour problems are commonly seen in survivors of traumatic brain injury during the course of their recovery. Gary initially started resisting when therapists tried to move his limbs, particularly his lower limb, which made it difficult for the therapists to perform their therapeutic exercise sessions. He took off his splints, and he refused to participate in his grooming sessions. Next, he began crying during his therapy sessions. Samira and the consultant talked to him about this: they wanted to ensure that Gary was not in pain. The conclusion was that the crying was a behavioural issue and not due to pain. It was essential to continue with the exercises to prevent deformities and contractures, but Gary's behaviour was hindering his participation in rehabilitation. An attempt was made to identify triggers that elicited problem behaviour. Frustration and agitation were observed to occur whenever Gary had difficulty expressing himself or when he could not accomplish certain tasks because of his limited vision, speech and mobility.

He was prompted and given clear instructions about the benefit of the exercises he needed to do from both Samira and Wendie. He was also given extra time to relax in the hope this would help him cope with the exercises. Wendie was asked to attend the sessions to observe Gary's behaviour and to encourage him in the therapy sessions. This proved helpful, as Gary appeared to listen to his mother. He was also referred to the visiting psychiatrist, whose report follows.

- His worsening memory and functional ability, together with increased mood lability coinciding with the post seizure period (coinciding with one of Gary's few seizures), suggest further brain injury as a result of the seizure.
- This, together with normal frustration exacerbated by poor cognitive function, means he does not always understand the therapeutic activities and cannot tolerate the concept of deferred benefit.
- He is not depressed at this time but is at risk of becoming so. While I have not prescribed antidepressants, they may become indicated if his emotional lability worsens and if negative cognitions associated with frustration, develop.
- Low dose antipsychotics may also be helpful in managing his labile mood but their use is cautioned because of the risk of sedation and the negative impact they might have on mobilisation and cognition. None were prescribed today but if deterioration occurs, they could be considered.

These drugs were never prescribed, and Gary's behaviour was managed through a behaviour-management programme.

Changes in behaviour following traumatic brain injury

Behaviour problems are common after TBI. Baguley, Cooper and Felmingham (2006) found that 25% of survivors of moderate to severe TBI were classified as aggressive. Agitation after traumatic brain injury (TBI) is the most frequently observed behavioural problem and arguably the greatest challenge to those providing rehabilitation. Research indicates that agitation is frequently found during recovery from severe brain injury (Angelino, Miglioretti, & Zotti, 2002). The empirical literature suggests that agitation occurs in approximately 64% of patients who have a severe brain injury, whereas agitation is only seen in 22% of those patients who have sustained a mild brain injury (Angelino et al., 2002; Bogner et al., 2001). It has been argued that the reason agitation is higher in severely brain injured patients is due to these patients having poor arousal or awareness after coma together with impaired cognition.

When considering antecedents of agitation in patients who have sustained a traumatic brain injury, it should be noted that cognitive impairment could be argued as being a key antecedent. As mentioned earlier, poor cognition including memory deficits, attention problems, loss of executive function and confusion and/or delirium are common after TBI (Davis, 2000; Lenzlinger, Morganti-Kossmann, Laurer, & McIntosh, 2001; Stuss et al., 1999). Together with poor arousal and awareness following coma and prolonged disorders of consciousness, the patient's ability to recognise environmental stimuli is significantly diminished. Kaplan and Kaplan (1982) highlight that people naturally have a fear of the unknown and show anxiety-based reactions in an unfamiliar environment. Given that many patients, following a severe TBI, are placed in unfamiliar rehabilitation centres or hospitals together with a lowered ability to recognise environmental stimuli, it is arguably not surprising that patients show signs of agitation and distress. This in turn becomes a challenge for the treating team.

As Gary started to emerge from a prolonged disorder of consciousness (i.e. minimally conscious state), he started to become more agitated and distressed. Gary started to exhibit signs of physical aggression in that he would hit out or kick therapists working with him, and later verbal aggression became apparent. Given the cited research, this was not seen as an uncommon experience, and the rehabilitation team treating Gary were well versed in dealing with behaviours such as agitation and aggression. As a result, a referral was made to Dr Anita Rose, consultant neuropsychologist, to assess and support the team in working with Gary.

Understanding challenging behaviour first requires recognising what the triggers are, that is to say what may or may not be contributing to the observed behaviour. Therefore, a behavioural analysis was begun and involved observation and data collection of Gary's behaviours in various settings and situations. It was reported that the majority of behavioural issues occurred during physiotherapy, neuro-functional therapy and personal care. Anita observed Gary in these situations and asked staff to complete ABC charts (where A = Antecedents, B = Behaviour and C = Consequence). This initial analysis was conducted over a week, and the frequency of behaviour (the number of times Gary exhibited agitation in any given situation) was measured. Information was also gathered about the particular situations in which most agitation occurred and how this was dealt with. After this initial assessment, a number of triggers were identified and included (1) pain; (2) Gary's perception he was being treated like a "child" (in NFR they used nursery rhymes to support rhythm of movement); (3) fear and anxiety at being hoisted/moved (due to paucity of his vision he was unable to see what was happening); and (4) being unsure where he was and who was with him (again this was due to his very poor vision).

Following a consultation with the neuropsychiatrist and the rest of the multidisciplinary team, it was felt that a behavioural intervention would be more beneficial than using a pharmacological intervention. Behavioural therapy intervention is an accepted approach to modifying behaviour following TBI (Alderman, 2003; Denmark & Gemeinhardt, 2002).

Agitation is often defined as one or more repetitive, non-purposeful and inappropriate verbal and/or motor behaviours. In the case of Gary, it was noted he displayed predominately motor behaviours in attempting to kick and hit staff. It was clear that external stimulation provoked his agitated behaviour, notably having poor vision and poor tolerance of physical touch. In addition, his cognitive impairment and emotional lability as he was emerging from MCS were contributing to this agitation. Research highlights that interventions for agitated behaviours are most effective before the peak level of agitation is reached (Hall & Buckwalter, 1987). Therefore, to ensure an environment for Gary in which agitation and distress were dealt with before a peak level was reached, staff were provided with behavioural guidelines to use when working with Gary. This ensured that a consistent approach was used and – given the numbers of staff involved in his care – this was imperative (see Table 11.1, Figure 11.2).

Table 11.1 Behavioural Guidelines

BEHAVIOURAL GUIDELINES FOR GARY HAYWARD

ALL STAFF TO FOLLOW GUIDELINES *AT ALL TIMES & ENSURE THESE ARE FOLLOWED TOGETHER WITH RISK ASSESSMENTS*

Reason: To have a consistent response during episodes of Gary's agitated behaviour in order to reduce the frequency of occurrence and to establish the most helpful way of responding to the behaviour.

Aim of Guidelines: To prevent the occurrence of inappropriate behaviour in order to improve quality of rehabilitation and to minimise the risk of untoward incident that may arise as a consequence of heightened level of agitation.

Step by Step Guidelines:

1. Gary has reduced vision so in approaching and interacting with Gary, start the conversation by telling him your name, who you are you are, and your role to establish rapport.
2. Keep in mind that he needs slow, clear and concise instructions to comprehend information and requires time to respond.
3. Always explain your intentions to Gary before beginning an activity and avoid sudden touching or grabbing. Explain in very brief terms what is going to happen. This can prevent a startle reaction that could lead to agitation. Remember Gary has poor vision so constant explanation is important.

(Continued)

Table 11.1 (Continued)

4. Throughout all interactions ensure you are always speaking in a calm manner and reassuring him at all times.
5. If he becomes physically aggressive i.e. biting, scratching, kicking respond by saying "No this is not acceptable", "I Don't Like this", or use a firm "No". ***NEVER RAISE YOUR VOICE WHEN RESPONDING.***
6. Give him clear feedback in a calm and encouraging voice such as "Ok I will leave you now just stay calm and relax" or "Gary you sound like you are upset, relax and I will let you have a rest".
7. Reassure Gary that you are supporting him and providing care for him that's why you are "changing him", "giving him his breakfast" etc. Always speak in a calm reassuring voice.
8. Do not carry on with given activities if Gary's mood is not stable and ensure that he is given time out in a safe place such as chair, wheelchair or bed. You may leave him for a few minutes but stay close i.e. within eye distance so you can see him although he is unable to see you.
9. Return and check whether Gary is ready to engage with the task. If not, determine why the activity is being refused and try to give him choices to know what he wanted and work it out.
10. If his mood is already settled and he is able to follow instructions give him positive feedback such as "Thank you for listening Gary" or "Gary you did a very good job". This will make him motivated to participate and kept engaged in an activity.
11. Formally end your time together informing Gary that you intend to leave or end a conversation. Therefore, it is important to state your intentions, "I have to leave now Gary". It is also important to give thanks and let him know when and what will be the next session to prepare him for the next meeting. When you use these general rules of contact, your interactions with Gary are likely to be smoother. There is less chance for agitation, restlessness or other behaviours to occur.

Following the implementation of the behavioural guidelines there was an initial improvement in Gary's agitation; however, this was short lived (Figure 11.2).

The second stage of the behavioural modification intervention was to employ strategies that staff could use in situ with Gary. The completed ABC charts and observational data highlighted that using distraction techniques appeared to have a positive effect when Gary became distressed, in particular when he was in pain. Therefore, Anita attended physiotherapy and NFR sessions with Gary over a period of 2 weeks and taught staff how to use breathing exercises with Gary. One staff member would be at the "head end" with Gary when he was in treatment, and whilst therapists conducted physical therapy, they would engage Gary with deep breathing exercises thereby distracting him and

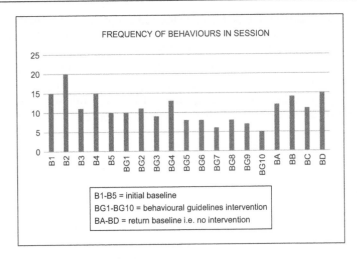

Figure 11.2 Changes in behaviour and use of behavioural guidelines

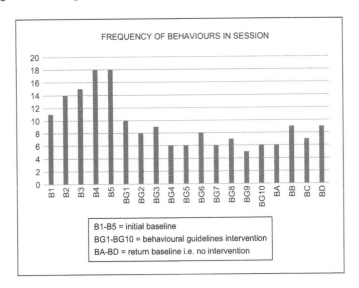

Figure 11.3 Changes in behaviour and use of distraction and deep breathing

enabling him to relax. These are both recognised techniques in anxiety and pain management. Following this, a significant improvement was noted (Figure 11.3). The improvement was maintained at return to baseline. Following this intervention, it was agreed to continue with both ensuring the behavioural guidelines were followed and the use of distraction and breathing to be used in physical sessions.

Gary quickly progressed through this stage of his recovery, and a significant and rapid change was noted in his level of agitation and distress.

The positive change as a result of the behavioural intervention used with Gary highlights the importance of rehabilitation staff being aware of and trained with dealing with challenging behaviours. They also need to understand the neurological process of recovery following TBI. In addition, it is imperative to have a consistent approach to modifying behaviours.

Regular review meetings were held and, at every meeting, Gary was continuing to improve. At almost 2 years after the assault, Gary was still receiving intensive rehabilitation. Physiotherapists collaborated with the doctors and the neurorehabilitation consultant to monitor the effects of medications administered for Gary's increased muscle tone. Over time, the tone in his lower left foot improved. This had a significant positive impact on his ability to transfer. Baclofen, a medication for spasticity, that is to say an increase in muscle tone, was discontinued. A soft cast splint for his left knee was discarded, too, as Gary was able to straighten his knee when relaxed. He continued to receive exercises in the prone position to improve his hip extension. Gary started to stand up from his wheelchair with moderate assistance from two people. He began to maintain good posture in the standing frame sessions. No external aids were required except for occasional reminders to maintain uprightness. His right ankle still required positioning to prevent an inward rotation of his ankle. Gary was referred for a surgical boot to improve weight bearing on his legs.

The behaviour problems reduced, and Gary began actively participating in the various therapeutic sessions. Although still variable, he was becoming much more cooperative and started to enjoy the sessions, as he showed through smiling, laughing, giggling and singing along with the therapist during his Padovan sessions. His memory was improving, too, as he started recalling the lyrics of the songs. These songs were therapeutic songs sung during the Padovan exercises. Gary had never heard these prior to his brain injury so must have learned them during the recovery phase. Facial exercises to improve his tongue control and facial expressions together with oral exercises to improve lung capacity recommenced.

The next problem encountered was that Gary started complaining about abdominal pain. This was thought to be due to a kidney stone, so, on July 31, 2013, Gary had further investigations. He was prescribed painkillers and was discharged back to the RMC with a tentative date for a nephrostomy in September. A nephrostomy is an artificial opening created between the kidney and the skin to allow for diversion of urine to a bag. Gary was further hospitalised for 10 days at a local hospital, as he pulled out a nephrostomy tube. On November 21, 2013, he was readmitted to the same unit for right ureteroscopy (an examination of the upper urinary tract) and laser removal of kidney stones. All patients with profound brain damage are unable to control their bladders. Urethral catheters are typically used to manage this, and such catheters encourage the development of kidney stones (Andrews, 2005).

In December 2013, Gary had his 31st birthday, and soon after it was Christmas. Although for the previous two birthdays and Christmases, Gary had seen his family, none of them were able to enjoy the good times because of his condition. This time Wendie did everything she could to make this a memorable day. Not only did she bring gifts, she also arranged for Gary's children to visit and sit on his lap while he was in his chair. That he cared for his children was obvious and touching to those who observed this. They felt he was lucky to have such a caring family, particularly his mother, Wendie, and his sister, Zowey.

Gary's right arm was still weak, especially in the upper compared to the lower joints. This caused him difficulty in performing overhead activities when he had to use both hands. His legs were weak, too, the right more than the left. His sitting balance, however, was good, so he no longer needed a tilt-in-space wheelchair to help him maintain sitting balance. The old wheelchair was discarded, and he was provided with an attendant-propelled, standard wheelchair. Regular physiotherapy and hydrotherapy sessions continued. His ability to transfer was improving, and he now only needed a little help from one person when transferring from bed to wheelchair and vice versa. Gary was able to lift up his pelvis once his right leg was stabilised. The improvement generalised to other skills such as dressing his lower body and changing his incontinence pads.

The next review from speech and language therapy noted that Gary's main communication problem was moderate to severe word-finding difficulties. He also had some expressive language impairments, for although his speech appeared to be fluent, it was lacking in content. Whenever Gary could not think of the word he wanted to say, he resorted to saying, "I don't know really. I don't know". This was his stock answer (also noted in his neuropsychological assessment report). Despite prompting, he gave up trying to communicate when he struggled to find the word he wanted. He tended not to initiate conversation and just to respond to other people questioning him. He wanted to participate in therapy, however. The speech and language therapists decided to formulate short-term goals to (1) improve Gary's word finding by facilitating spontaneous use of supportive strategies and (2) to increase Gary's initiation of conversation with staff and members of his family. To achieve the first short-term goal, Gary was engaged in a number of tasks which made him think of a particular word. He was asked to think whether the word could be an object, a season, a verb, an adjective or so forth. Whenever Gary appeared to be struggling to think of a specific word, the therapist cued Gary by describing the item and/or giving him the initial letter of the word. The aim of this was for Gary to be able to self-prompt when he was struggling to think of the words or, alternatively, think of another way of saying what he meant. He was also provided with scenarios to practise initiating conversation and taking turns in conversations. He slowly began to improve in both areas. His object naming and sentence completion abilities markedly improved, and he required less prompting. The nursing staff reported that he was beginning to initiate conversations. He began to contribute to conversations as well as responding to specific questions.

Improvements were also noticed in functional areas. Gary progressed from needing maximum assistance to only requiring minimal assistance in most of the activities of daily living. He was now having meals of normal consistency. He still required supervision because of the possibility of seizures and, because of his poor vision, he also needed help to chop food into pieces and to pour liquid in a cup. He tended to use his left hand for most tasks and needed prompting to use his right hand to stabilise objects, such as using a fork or holding the cup while he was drinking. He became completely independent in his swallowing and was managing many tasks safely.

Intensive rehabilitation enabled Gary to achieve increased functional independence. A further goal was formulated, namely for Gary to be able to go home for weekends to visit his family and to be able to re-integrate into his own community. The occupational therapists carried out home visits and made recommendations as well as providing risk assessments. By now, Gary had functional use of both his upper limbs and also had good muscle strength in the left side with fair muscle strength in his right side, being able to manage grooming, showering and dressing. He was still blind in his left eye, although able to see colours and shadows from the right corner of his right eye. He still needed total assistance in shaving and set-up assistance in brushing his teeth (his toothpaste had to be placed on his toothbrush). He could wash his face, comb his hair and wash his hands safely and independently when the equipment was set up with the supervision of one person. When showering, he used a shower chair because of the weakness in his legs, but he only needed minimal assistance to wash, rinse and dry his chest, abdomen, both arms, his front perineal area and his left leg. This was closely supervised by the occupational therapist and/or the rehabilitation assistant because of the risk of a seizure.

The rehabilitation assistant reported a reduction in the frequency of bladder and bowel incontinence, as by now Gary was more aware of urination and defecation and called for the bedpan whenever he felt the urge to urinate. He then began to request the urinal bottle and asked the staff to keep it next to him so he could use it on his own. On his own initiative, he started to ring the nurses' alarm to catch the nurses' attention when his bottle needed emptying or when he felt the need to open his bowels. Consequently, bowel accidents reduced.

Gary became more alert and aware of his surroundings. In the first months of 2014, he showed improvements in speech, expression, orientation and concentration. He was assessed with the Montreal Cognitive Assessment (MOCA-blind) for his cognition. This was used because of his poor vision. He was oriented to person, place and situation and was recognising familiar voices. His immediate memory was good, although his recall of recent events such as recall of attendance at therapy sessions, recent family visits and remembering what he had eaten for lunch was not so good. His long-term memory was fair so that when presented with three choices, he could accurately recall his address, his date of birth and other events. He was reasonably good at recalling names of his family members but had difficulty recalling the names of members of staff who worked closely with him even when given cues and prompts such as the initial letter. Having been a right hander, Gary now held the pen in his left hand when trying to write his name. Although legible, the letters overlapped because of his poor vision.

Chapter 12

Home evaluation

In order to prepare for Gary's discharge, it was essential that the team at the Raphael assessed the living quarters which would be his home for the foreseeable future. A visit to determine accessibility was an important step in the discharge planning for Gary's move from inpatient care to his mother's home. The visit offered an insight into what goals needed to be worked on for a safe and successful discharge. Although Gary had re-learned to perform various activities of daily living with assistance within the rehabilitation setting, the access visit therapist, Samira, noted his difficulty in carrying over these tasks in a different and perhaps less protected environment. At the time of the visit in November 2013, Wendie's house had not yet been adapted for his safe discharge. Other objectives of the access visit were to assess and identify the following:

1. accessibility needs in terms of type of equipment and modalities to be used at home;
2. if modifications and structural adaptations were needed to make the house accessible and viable as a place of care for short home visits and for future discharge;
3. wheelchair accessibility in the home;
4. safety concerns;
5. risk factors in the home environment allowing safe and effective care at home.

Wendie wanted Gary to be at home over Christmas for at least a few hours. Gary also wished to return home following discharge from rehabilitation. The family lived in a two-story house, having recently moved. The accessibility assessment took into account Gary's current condition as well as considering any future progress he might make. Wheelchair dependency and relevant accessibility was, therefore, the top priority.

All areas of the house Gary was going to live in were assessed. These comprised the entrance, the hallway, the living room, the bathroom, the kitchen and the dining room. Samira carried out the assessment in the presence of Wendie. She began by determining how Gary would enter the house. Measurements of the physical features in the environment, including door frames, chair and sofa heights, the height of the commode from the floor, the location of door knobs and so forth, were taken in order to determine if each aspect of the house would be accessible to Gary while he was seated in his wheelchair. Such detailed assessment was essential to make recommendations for adaptive equipment together with rearrangement of items or addition or removal of items and whether Gary would be safe living with his family after his discharge from the rehabilitation centre or during weekend visits.

Assessment and recommendation

Although Gary would be able to access his house using the front entrance, as the door was wide enough, with a suitable reach for using the door lock, there was insufficient space once inside the door to manoeuvre his wheelchair and perform 90-degree turns. Such space was essential, as Gary had to access the downstairs living area. It was recommended that a C-shaped ramp should be installed to enable Gary to access his living room. A detailed report was forwarded to the Social Services OT team for further recommendations. Once the ramp was installed, Gary would be able to enter the house safely.

Figure 12.1 Wendie and Gary 2014

Interior of the home

Overall, there was sufficient lighting for Gary to see objects and entrances and manoeuvre himself around the home. The light switches were easily accessible, and there was nothing in the floor area of the hallway to increase the risk of falls.

Living room

The living room was carpeted, with one loose removable rug and two sofas of appropriate heights. The size of this living area was sufficient to convert into a possible micro-environment for Gary's bedroom. Once the loose rugs had been removed, the area would be wheelchair friendly. The actual bedroom was located on the first floor, and as there was no stair lift and Gary needed a wheelchair, it was unsafe for him to access this floor, so Samira recommended that the existing living room should be converted into Gary's bedroom.

Hallway

The width of the hall was sufficient to enable a wheelchair to be manoeuvred. Although it became narrower when it met the downstairs kitchen, Gary would still be able to access it without obstruction.

Stairway

The stairs to the first landing were immediately to the left after entering the front door. There were 13 steps, each 7.78 centimetres tall, with stair rails on either side and sufficient lighting at the top and bottom of the stairs. Gary was unable to use the stairs, however, as he was dependent on his wheelchair for mobility. The bathroom was upstairs, yet Gary needed to be able to access essential bathing facilities in order to maintain his self-care. A stair lift was possible, and there was room for this, but the area would need to be assessed and the lift eventually provided by the occupational therapy team from Social Services.

Bedroom

This was located on the first landing and contained a single bed and a small table. Despite being wheelchair friendly, Gary was unable to use it because of his inability to get upstairs.

Bathroom and toilet

Gary was unable to access the bathroom and toilet, as this was located upstairs. Because of this, Samira recommended that Gary strip-wash downstairs until he was assessed for a stair lift by the Social Services team. In addition, she suggested a wet room should be installed in the downstairs living area. Meanwhile, Gary would require a mobile commode chair and urinal bottle in order for him to manage his personal care needs on a temporary basis. The other temporary option was for Gary to shower at the Raphael Medical Centre, as his house was only a 5-minute drive away. This option was the one Gary and Wendie chose.

Kitchen/dining area

The kitchen was located at the end of the hallway, which then led into the dining room. Gary was able to access this with his wheelchair for dining with his family. The dining room contained one large dining table with a suitable height and enough space to allow Gary's wheelchair to fit underneath. He could sit on the dining chairs but, as they did not have arm rests or seatbelts, he would require close supervision.

Inside home safety

There was no existing emergency alarm in place within the home, and Gary was unable to independently leave in the case of a fire or other emergency. Smoke and carbon monoxide detectors had already been fitted into the house. The provision of a nursing alarm was therefore recommended.

Conclusions and recommendations

In the light of the accessibility assessment, a number of recommendations were made, as outlined in each section. Gary was continuing to make progress, however, so in order to maximise his potential for maintaining independence at home, various adjustments/structural changes were necessary and should be put in place as soon as possible to enable a satisfactory return home. These were:

All living spaces

• Remove all loose rugs from the living areas and carpet edges in order to reduce the risk of falls/hazards.

- Additionally, remove low furniture and floor objects and reduce any existing clutter around the home.
- Secure the carpet or treads on the stairs (this was mostly for the safety of other family members).

Front home access

- A small ramp should be installed (preferably C shaped) in order for Gary to access his home independently and negotiate the existing 5-inch threshold leading into the property.

Access to bedroom

- As Gary was unable to access his upstairs bedroom, he would need to have a C-shaped ramp installed near the beginning of the hallway in order to access his temporary bedroom. Wendie should order a hospital profiling bed, in case Gary would like to rest on his short visit (3–4 hours). It was essential that the Social Services team look further into this.

Access to suitable bathing facilities

- Gary was not able to access suitable bathing facilities, as these were located upstairs.
- **OPTION 1:** It was recommended that a wet room should be installed in the downstairs living area or on a temporary basis. He could use the mobile commode chair and urinal bottle in the living room, as this would be his temporary bedroom.
- **OPTION 2:** Gary should be assessed by the Social Services team for a possible stair lift to access the available bedroom, bathroom and toilet.

A further visit was made 8 months after the first visit. During this visit (in July 2014), Gary was accompanied by Wendie and Samira from the Raphael Medical Centre. The aim of this visit was to assess whether (1) the new profiling bed was adequate and (2) the amount of space available allowing for safe transfers on and off the bed was adequate.

Assessment findings

On arrival, the profiling bed was assessed to see that all its functions were working appropriately. These were all satisfactory. There was adequate space for transfers to take place once the clutter at the side of the room was removed. Following this, Gary was brought into the room and positioned 90 degrees to the side of the bed, ready to transfer. Wendie removed the left side of the wheelchair, creating clear access for Gary to transfer independently onto the bed. He was then able to safely transfer and reposition himself appropriately on the bed with no problem. Gary was then asked to transfer back onto the wheelchair, which he also did safely and acceptably with no major concerns.

Recommendations

- Gary would require someone to support and prompt him as and when required for each transfer on and off the bed.
- It was essential to ensure that the area around the bed was clutter free, with no trip hazards or distractions.
- The height of the bed should be adjusted to the correct level, and the bed's functions should be utilised appropriately to assist with standing transfers back to the wheelchair and/or commode.

Chapter 13

Gary today

In August 2014, Gary began short visits home (to his mother's house), where he spent a few hours. By September, he was visiting home every day, and on October 14, he started a trial of sleeping at home. At the time of writing, January 2015, he is still sleeping at home and attends the RMC 5 to 6 mornings a week for ongoing rehabilitation and showering. Wendie would have taken him home before but had to wait for a hospital bed. Her father, who has dementia, also lives with her. (She had to wait several months to get a hospital bed for him, too). The bed arrived but the house has not yet been adapted for Gary. The bathroom is upstairs and, as Gary cannot manage the stairs, he cannot have a shower or a bath at home. Wendie had started taking Gary out for walks about 6 months after his admission to the RMC before he regained consciousness. She explained that the staff encouraged her to take Gary out for a walk early on, but she was nervous. She said, *"They kept saying 'Take him out, take him out'. I said 'Where do I take him?' They said 'Take him out for a walk'. I said 'No, no, the chair might go over, I might knock the chair over'. I was so frightened of taking him out. I was nervous, you know. What if something happened? What if he had a seizure? I don't know how to deal with all that. It was a long time before I felt confident. Then we started coming out in the garden on our own"*.

Gary's daughter Kelsey added, *"Yeah and having picnics"*.

Wendie continued, *"Yeah, we had picnics out there and played in the garden with the kids and we had races as well. In April 2014, we started to think about overnight stays, maybe a weekend. Gerhard (the head of the RMC) gave permission to keep him one night, take him home, but because the bed wasn't ready, the bed I've got wasn't suitable. We've got to have a hospital one which is fine. He's home a lot now although he sleeps at the Raphael. We started planning to get him home in August 2013. He came home for Christmas Day. That was his first day home, Christmas Day 2013. That was the first time he came in the house"*.

Her granddaughter reminded her, *"It was the first time you actually celebrated Christmas".*

Wendie went on, *"Yeah, because I hadn't been able to celebrate Christmas. I said I wouldn't celebrate Christmas until he came home. No Christmas Day or anything for the previous two years".*

When Gary was asked to tell us about himself now, he said, *"Since I woke up, I've improved big time. I like a joke and a laugh, I can see the funny side of things, that's what makes people like me. I am a serious person, a family person. I don't talk to my children about what happened and how I am now. I know they love me, I know that. One eye still doesn't work. I cope with glasses but my sight is not good enough to drive".*

On January 18, 2014, Gary gave his first interview to the *Croydon Advertiser* since the attack. Chief reporter Gareth Davies heard that Gary was determined to make a full recovery even though he had no memory of the events of that night.

Croydon Advertiser report (January 18, 2014):

'TWO years ago Gary Hayward was clinging to life, unable to respond to his family's pleas for him to wake up. Now the father of three is laughing and joking and has amazed them with his progress. "I'm getting stronger every day and I'm going to make a full recovery", he said. "I'm going to destroy every obstacle in my way".

'Gary, 31, was beaten with metal poles and pieces of wood while protecting his father John from a gang of around 30 teenagers in Central Parade, New Addington, on October 2, 2011.

As well as being in an unresponsive state for 18 months, the brutal attack – for which no one has been caught – left Gary blind in one eye, with next to no sight in the other.

He was unable to walk or move the right side of his body and suffered severe memory loss.

This week he was able to shake hands with the reporter who visited him and his mum, Wendie Hayward, at a specialist rehabilitation centre in Kent.

The improvement from a little over six months ago, when he said his first words since that night, is stunning.

It is matched only by how remarkably positive he is about the ordeal he has been through.

Asked about his eyesight, Gary said: "I can see colours and figures, but I can't make out faces or anything like that. It doesn't worry me though. I've been told that I will see eventually".

As well as being able to have a conversation, it is clear his personality, especially his sense of humour, has returned.

Throughout the interview he joked with his mother as she nagged him about being impatient, demanding extra physiotherapy sessions or being rude to the nurses.

It's the sort of thing most mums and sons take for granted, but for Wendie, who has visited Gary every day since the attack, they are precious moments she feared they might not have again.

"What do you think of the food here Gary?" she asked.

"It's horrible", he replied, laughing.

"He tells them that too", said Wendie.

"He was always this blunt. We're seeing a lot of the old Gary now. He's very comical. His wit is coming back. He's getting his one-liners in".

His love of music has also returned. When we arrived, Gary was listening to music on the CD/DVD player he got for Christmas.

When asked who the singer was, Gary replied: "Phil Collins. I also like Pink Floyd, Queen, AC-DC, loads of stuff.

"I've got five CDs, and they're all what I like. I've listened to them over and over again, but that's alright".

"He knew all the words when he first started listening", added Wendie.

"I think [his interest in music] was the first thing he responded to. We constantly played music while he was in a coma".

Gary, surprised, said: "Did you? Bloody hell"!

As well as his favourite bands, Gary is able to recall his children and the rest of his close family, along with small details such as the number of his house and the street where he lived in New Addington.

What he cannot remember yet is his life before that night – his childhood, growing up, the birth of his children – or the attack itself.

"I got beaten up by 30 people", he said. "I can't remember any names yet".

Wendie said: "We won't tell him too many details because we want him to remember on his own.

"He doesn't remember the attack and, in some ways, I don't want him to. Who would want to remember being hit with hammers and poles?"

"He doesn't remember being asleep either, so all those hours I spent here were a waste of time", she laughed.

Walking continues to be a major obstacle but, with the help of regular physiotherapy sessions, he has made progress and is almost able to support his own weight without help.

So keen is he to get back on his feet, he has demanded extra sessions.

He is making huge strides since last June, when he said "hello" to his sister Zowey over the phone, his first words since the attack.

Last month the *Advertiser* revealed that Gary was well enough to spend time at his mum's house over the festive period.

This week he described spending Christmas with his family as "pukka".

Wendie has moved to Kent to be closer to her son.

The plan now is for him to leave rehab within the next few months.

In the long term he wants to return to New Addington and live with his children in a place of his own.

"I would definitely want to go back", he said. "It's the only place I know".

Asked whether he realised that he was thought of as a hero by his family for protecting his dad, he said: "I wouldn't say that".

"We think you're a hero", said Wendie, before giving him a big hug.

Mother's torment

WENDIE Hayward has described how close she came to losing her son.

"He died in the ambulance on the way to hospital but they brought him back to life", she said.

"Did I? Me?" asked Gary. "Bloody Nora"!

Wendie said: "When we got to the hospital the surgeon came out to us and said we needed to decide whether or not to operate.

"If we didn't he would die, but if they did the chances are he would be brain damaged.

"He said we should do what Gary would want us to do and to think of him, and whether he would be happy being paralysed.

"I know he wouldn't have wanted to be like that, but I still said yes to the operation.

"I was selfish that night because I wanted him to live.

"It was lucky I did, because he would have been gone. He's proof there's always a chance".

Gary said: "I think that's marvellous".

Investigation met wall of silence

GARY was beaten with pieces of wood and metal poles after confronting youths who had been harassing his father in Central Parade in New Addington.

Four people have been arrested but no one has been charged with the attack.

Police believe they know who was responsible but despite numerous appeals by his family, a £20,000 reward and a feature on BBC's *Crimewatch*, aired in April last year, no witnesses have agreed to give evidence in court.

In August, Borough Commander David Musker revealed the investigation has been shelved because there were "no further viable leads".

"The fundamental issue has always been identifying a witness or witnesses present at the scene that would be willing to provide a statement and identify the persons involved", he said.

When asked whether he thought he was a different person now or the same Gary as he was before, he replied, "I'm different. I used to take a lot of weed, cannabis and now I don't touch it. I am completely drug free. Mind you, I was told that was the reason I survived the attack. I had just had a joint when I went out and that made me relaxed. Otherwise I might not have survived".

Printed with permission of the *Croydon Advertiser*.

More from the Raphael staff

From November 2014, Gary had regular sessions with the assistant psychologist, Lisha, who helped him with his college application. The following is a summary of her sessions with him.

Lisha's first session with Gary was on November 4, 2014. They discussed his desire to return to work and to obtain some qualifications in wiring. Gary had no General Certificate of Secondary Education (GCSE) certificates or other school-leaving qualifications. Together they did some internet searches to understand the eligibility criteria for undertaking a wiring course, and ascertained that work experience is acceptable in place of GCSEs. As they were unable to find a course focused exclusively on wiring, Lisha agreed to do some research to find a course which had a focus on wiring.

On November 11, 2014, Lisha showed Gary a level 1 electrical installation course at a college in Gillingham. She explained that although there were no courses focused exclusively on wiring, there was a module in the syllabus focussed on electrical installation. Gary appeared interested in the course and said he would call the college to discuss the course and whether it was suitable for him. He was not concerned about the distance as he was confident he would be walking by the time the course began. Gary made the call during his session with Lisha. It became apparent that Gary was likely to forget what he needed to say/ask. Gary and Lisha then created a list of questions he would like to ask the college (see what follows) to facilitate Gary's memory. It was agreed that Gary would take the lead on the call, with Lisha taking notes of the conversation for further discussion.

In this session, Gary once again said he wanted to return to work, as he was feeling a bit 'useless' at home. Lisha and Gary agreed to start working on his CV as a starting point. Gary promised to bring dates and names of his previous employers in the next session.

Questions/information for college:

1. Gary to briefly explain his current situation and learning needs to the college (TBI, memory deficits, blindness in left eye, wheelchair user).
2. He would ask about support for people like him.
3. And how much the course would cost.
4. He also needed to know the closing dates for applications.
5. And whether he could do the course and work at the same time.

On November 18, 2014, Gary planned to make the call to the college. He used a laptop and, with some help from Lisha, acquired the contact details for the college. Gary successfully completed the phone call and gathered the required information with minimal assistance. The call was made on a speaker phone so Lisha could make notes on the information provided by the college. When the call was completed, Gary felt very pleased at doing this independently. He said this was the first time he had made a call to an unknown external person since the assault. He then accessed the college website to begin the application process. He agreed to work on his personal statement for the application in the next session.

Gary provided Lisha with the details of his work history and agreed to begin building his CV further in order to complete the college application. In this session, Gary was excited, because on the following day, November 19, 2014, he was due for a foot operation which would allow him to begin walking again. The following week, however, on November 25, he was low and disappointed because the foot operation had been cancelled. Alternative transport options to get to and from college were discussed together with the possibility of returning to work as a wheelchair user. Gary, though, was determined to walk again, and his mood appeared to lift as work on his personal statement commenced.

Gary and Lisha worked on his personal statement together. Gary typed this into the college application independently. As the application was not finished, it was agreed that the final stages of the application form would be completed in the next session.

However, Gary was unable to attend the next two sessions because of various appointments to discuss the operation on his foot, with one doctor saying the operation was not possible and would not enable Gary to walk. When next seen on December 15, 2014, he expressed frustration and disappointment at the slow progress and the clinicians' opinions of the operation.

Gary accessed the college site, completed the application form and submitted it. He reported feeling very pleased at having done this and said he felt excited about going on a course and getting life started again. He reported looking forward to meeting new people and making friends, as well as to being able to return to work. Gary was to now expect a phone call from the college to discuss his learning needs and to invite him for an interview. It was decided to begin building on his CV at the next session.

On January 6, 2015, a call was made to the college to enquire about the status of Gary's application, and plans were made to visit the college to see how long it took to get there and to see the site. Meanwhile, Lisha and Gary started working on his CV together. This continued during the next two sessions.

On January 27, 2015, Gary called the college to enquire about visiting the campus. The visit was arranged for February 10, 2015. On this date, Lisha and Gary visited the college. He appeared pleased with the campus and the wiring workshop. He spoke to the course tutors and explained his background in the industry. He was informed by the college staff that he was supposed to have gone for an interview the previous month, whereupon Gary said he had not received the letter inviting him to the interview. Although he liked the college, Gary expressed some concerns about the age of the other students and felt that he might be too old for the course. The tutor pointed out that the ages of the other students ranged from 16 to 50 years. This appeared to soothe Gary's concerns. He discussed the distance of the college from his home and was worried about getting there, as he had not had the foot operation. Various other options for travel were discussed.

On February 17, 2015, Gary brought in a letter from the college enquiring about details of his learning needs. These were completed during his session with some assistance from Lisha. Gary asked Anita, the neuropsychologist, about acquiring a report on his learning needs and medication. He also called the college to discuss rescheduling another interview because he had missed the first one. The following week, he told Lisha that the college had telephoned, inviting him to an interview. Gary was unable to remember the date but reported that the college was going to send a letter with more details. He agreed to commence interview practise once the date was known. Although pleased with the progress, Gary had ongoing concerns of the impact of being a wheelchair user on his future. At the time of writing (March 2015), Gary had just learned that the operation on his foot is to take place the next month. Gary has now had the surgery and is learning to walk again. He has decided not to go to college because the travelling time is too great.

Chapter 14

Why did Gary do so well?

When Gary was first seen by the current authors, none of us predicted he would do well. He was in a vegetative state and remained so for a long time. Only a minority of people regain full consciousness after such a long period, and very few recover as well as Gary. It is well recognised that patients who are in a VS following anoxic damage do less well than those whose VS follows TBI (Giacino & Whyte, 2005; Guérit 2005; Kotchoubey 2005). Anoxia appears to result in irreversible neuronal loss. Andrews (2005) lists five conditions which should be provided to promote optimal recovery for patients with profound brain damage. These are:

1. Provide the optimal environment.
2. Prevent and treat secondary complications.
3. Include in treatment physiotherapy and the other "therapies", medical, psychological and technological.
4. Support the family.
5. Modify the environment, including regulating the amount of stimulation.

It is certainly the case that all these conditions were met in Gary's rehabilitation programme.

We know too that people denied rehabilitation do not do well (Elliott & Walker, 2005). Rusk and colleagues (1966) followed up 25 survivors of brain injury 5 to 15 years after they were considered unsuitable for rehabilitation. Five had died, and of the 18 patients still alive, there were "hundreds of incidents of infections and respiratory complications. Contractures were evident in all patients even those initially without contractures" (Elliott & Walker, 2005, p. 482).

We asked several people why they thought Gary had done so well. Wendie, his mother, considered it was tender, loving care, perseverance and not giving up, together with the staff and people at the Raphael Medical Centre. She recognised that most people do not have the same rehabilitation opportunities as her son. She told us that if he had gone into a home, he would probably be sitting hunched up in his wheelchair all day.

On January 14, 2015, the director of the RMC, Dr Gerhard Florschutz, was asked why he felt Gary had done so well. This is a transcript of the interview.

BW: Why do YOU think Gary did better than many people predicted?

GF: Well, it's very difficult to say, but if you look at the pathway, the history of his recovery, there was a pronounced difference after his cranioplasty, and I think since the cranioplasty he made progress that he wasn't able to make before. Then, of course, there was the input of the interdisciplinary team working very intensively with him, not just the physiotherapists but all the other therapists working with him, occupational therapy, neuropsychology and so on. That made a difference. The synergy of these various therapies really makes a difference.

BW: Have you seen other people like Gary? How unusual do you think he is?

GF: Well, he's very unusual. When one looks at his history, at the degree of his injury and the trauma and the length of his coma, I would say it's quite unusual. I mean we have had one or two other cases of a similar nature that have made an almost total recovery. Again, it's unexplainable why that happens.

BW: Do you think his family had anything to do with this?

GF: The mother most certainly was very important, and one can't underestimate her input. She was so motivating to him, pushing him and pushing herself as well, in a most positive way, that was very helpful.

BW: The other thing about Gary is that he failed to show improvement for such a long time that in normal circumstances, he would have been sent to a nursing home, and I feel that if that had happened he would have ended up very contracted (having permanent shortening of muscles or joints). Is that what you feel?

GF: Yes, that is really a lesson we have to bring to the attention of the funders. In many cases, they have to give space and time for recovery to take place. Then, in economic terms, the benefits would have been obvious. He would have been a cost to the health service to the end of his life. Now he will cease to have health funding needs very shortly. So from that point of view, neurorehabilitation is cost effective. He is a good example. That is really the problem that this medical orthodoxy has: that declares that after 6 months you are in a "persistent vegetative state" and after a year you are in a "permanent vegetative state" is nonsense. There are so many examples where people make recovery and improve long after that time. What we have to develop is a system where we can detect possibilities for recovery. How can we detect early on who can make a better recovery? That is a real research question. That is something we really have to work on.

BW: Well, that's an interesting one, but I don't know that it's possible. You know that Agnes Shiel, in her PhD in 1999, found five different patterns of recovery. One group remained vegetative while another group remained flat for a long time and then recovered. Gary would fit into this group. Then there were other patterns. The point of that study was that you couldn't predict which ones were going to do well in the first few months.

GF: With Gary, in one way, you could have predicted he would do well because of the cranioplasty. There are enough data now that, after a cranioplasty, enough people make a recovery, some more than others. This is one thing we can look at. [See Chapter 8 on cranioplasty in this book.]

BW: The other thing about cranioplasty is the timing. Some people, for example in Germany, think you have to do it quickly, whereas in the UK people tend to wait. Is it just money or risk of infection or what?

GF: The risk of infection is there anyway whenever you do it. If I'm being cynical, I think it's because they are waiting for them to die so they don't have to pay for it. It's almost as cruel as that. It makes sense to do it quickly because if you really want to encourage plasticity of the brain, you have to have a properly enveloped skull to function better. That is often the reason why people recover better after a cranioplasty.

BW: How close was Gary's waking up to the cranioplasty? It was quite a while afterwards, wasn't it?

GF: Quite soon I think.

[The cranioplasty was carried out in August 2012, and Gary emerged from the MCS in April 2013, 9 months later, but he did appear to be more awake after the cranioplasty.]

Anita Rose: I think there were some changes in his behaviour, he became more alert, and that was quite soon afterwards. [In fact, Gary emerged from the VS into the MCS soon after the cranioplasty.]

Samira also reminded us that Gary had remained physically well while at the RMC; he had not developed infections; which can often pull people down. There had been no further falls; his medication had been regularly reviewed; he had relatively few seizures, he never developed pressure sores and good nutrition and hydration had been maintained. Thus, his physical state had been the best it could have been, thus encouraging any recovery to take place. Wilson, Graham and Watson (2005) are among others who stress the importance of good physical care and the need to deal with treatable problems during the VS. They mention how patients who are heavily sedated can show improvement once the medications are stopped or adjusted.

Our colleague Lindsay McLellan, a neurologist and former professor of rehabilitation, when asked why he felt Gary had done so well, sent the following comments by email on February 10, 2015:

1. I think the mechanism of the initial injury was significant in that his head was likely to have been relatively stationary when hit (thus unlike a motorist travelling at speed); moreover the blow fractured the skull which thus absorbed some of the force of the blow and caused less catastrophic injury to the brain than initially thought.

2. Hydrocephalus is a very significant complicating factor; I suspect that current methods of assessment of the need to reduce intracranial pressure in an individual are insufficiently precise. The standard way of evaluating clinically whether a permanent shunt is needed to reduce the pressure is in my opinion lacking in subtlety and is far, far too brief, so that some people who would benefit from a permanent shunt are not given one. Once excess pressure is relieved, it may be several weeks or even months before clinical improvement appears and further improvement may then continue for 2 to 3 years and confound earlier predictions. (I have seen one such striking case similar to Gary's, that occurred in response to long term input from his family following decompression). Sometimes it takes a surgical procedure such as replacement of a bone flap to trigger the process of long term decompression and I suspect hydrocephalus was a significant factor in Gary's case, given his high level of eventual cognitive recovery. [In support of McLellan's view, Pickard and colleagues (2005) suggested that in vegetative patients, hydrocephalus is less likely to present as raised intracranial pressure and more likely to present as failure to improve.]

3. In addition, I am sure rehabilitation is crucially important. I think that a small proportion of individuals who are clinically unresponsive are actually aware as if in a dream but lack awareness of their ability to respond or comment, as

though stuck in 'watching TV' mode. They can eventually be encouraged out of this by a combination of specific physical arousal (as occurs during physiotherapy) and personal and cheerful appeals to respond which may need to be theatrically exaggerated (rather as parents intuitively adopt when encouraging young children). However, such responses may initially be very short lived, fatigue rapidly and be easy to miss. So frequent short inputs from someone sensitive to subtle changes are more effective than relatively infrequent 45 minute sessions. By contrast, I suspect that simply leaving people continuously attached to headphones or parked next to interminable TV induces a state of withdrawal from stimulation and thus delays recovery.

Another colleague, Agnes Shiel, the senior author of the WHIM, also sent an email on February 12, 2015, in which she wrote:

"Leaving aside the obvious explanations such as medication, nutritional status etc., which will have been considered, there is no obvious answer. It may be due to a combination of factors including careful assessment which identifies subtle signs of improvement leading to appropriate types and intensities of intervention. Another possible factor may be persistence in intervention – in many cases, rehabilitation is time limited and, where there is no obvious response after a given time, the focus changes to management and long term care. Perhaps some people with potential for improvement require persistent intervention over time in order to begin responding and simply do not get this opportunity, as Gary did here at the Raphael. A second factor may be readiness to respond and it could be that, serendipitously for some people, this readiness coincides with their access to rehabilitation. However, for many people with a Disorder of Consciousness, once the initial assessment and rehabilitation is completed, they are moved to continuing care where regular intervention if available at all is of a much lower intensity. Because no change is expected, the person is not challenged and therefore no change occurs. This case illustrates that for some individuals (albeit probably a minority) significant recovery is possible and can be maximised in a favourable environment".

Borthwick (2005) reminds us that patients described as being in the permanent or persistent VS **do** sometimes recover and that a paper on treatment decisions for VS patients from the *British Medical Journal* (Andrews, Murphy, Munday, & Littlewood, 1996) said the reported recovery of some of these patients was a cause for concern. Kotchoubey (2005) explains that VS patients may have islands of cortical activity but that these are disconnected from one another. In other words, there may be "lack of activity of large distributed cortical networks despite intact cortical activity" (ibid., p. 349). Wilson, Graham and Watson (2005) highlight the fact that there are some VS patients who show isolated behavioural fragments. Katchoubey (2005) tells us that there are two subtypes of VS, one with relatively intact thalamo-cortical links and one without. Gary presumably belonged to the former subtype. Rappoport (2005) also describes two subtypes of VS, namely "vegetative state" and "extreme vegetative state". Once again, Gary would appear to be in the former subtype.

Let us return to the patterns of recovery mentioned (Shiel, 1999). Using the WHIM, Shiel identified five different patterns of recovery in survivors of severe brain injury: (1) little evidence of change; (2) slow, steady progress; (3) rapid progress with a quick plateau; (4) initial rapid recovery, then slow progress; and (5) little if any progress at first, then steady progress for a long period. These patients, however, were in the acute stage. What about patients who remain unaware for many months? Dhamapurkar, Wilson, Rose and Florschutz (2015) wanted to know if the same patterns of recovery were seen in chronic patients using the same measures as Shiel (1999). They looked at 29 patients surviving severe brain injury who were in a VS or a MCS for several months. All were assessed regularly with the WHIM (Gary was one of the patients included in this study). Three of the participants had died. Of the remaining patients, 17 showed little evidence of change (Shiel's group 1). Three showed gradual improvement over time (Shiel's group 2). Two patients improved and then plateaued early (Shiel's group 3). Only one patient rapidly improved (Shiel's group 4). The final three patients were slow to start and then showed a marked improvement (similar to Shiel's group 5). Gary was one of these. The authors concluded that the taxonomy suggested by Shiel (1999) also appears to apply to patients in the chronic phase but with a delayed start of several months. They recognised that the findings need to be replicated with a larger group of patients. Guérit (2005) also mentions different patterns of recovery seen after TBI as measured by EEG.

One final point to make here is to remember Rosenblum (2015), mentioned in the recovery section in Chapter 3, who says that recovery after long periods of coma is possible if the critical connections between the brainstem and the ascending arousal system are intact. Gary did not have significant damage to the brainstem, and this may have contributed to his good outcome.

To quote Province (2005), "The customarily grim view of severe brain injury resulting in cognitive impairment provides a disincentive for the development and implementation of rehabilitation strategies that could benefit these patients" (p. 269). Gary is an example of how the principle of *never giving up* has led to a good quality of life for one such patient.

Postscript

Just as this book was to be submitted (late March 2015), Wendie received a letter from the police. She had made a complaint about the way Gary's case had been dealt with in May 2013. The reply was dated March 24, 2015. The police sergeant writing the letter admitted that Gary's case had been mishandled and that the officer in charge of the case at the time of the assault had breached professional standards. He would be subject to internal disciplinary procedures, and the service the Hayward family received did not meet the minimum standards required. Wendie is hoping that the case will be reopened.

References

Aarabi, B., Hesdorffer, D. C., Ahn, E. S., Aresco, C., Scalea, T. M., & Eisenberg, H. M. (2006). Outcome following decompressive craniectomy for malignant swelling due to severe head injury. *Journal of Neurosurgery, 104,* 469–479.

Agner, C., Dujovny, M., & Gaviria, M. (2002). Neurocognitive assessment before and after cranioplasty. *Acta Neurochirurgica (Wien), 144,* 1033–1040.

Ahmed, A. I., Eynon, C. A., Kinton, L., Nicoll, J. A., & Belli, A. (2010). Decompressive craniectomy for acute disseminated encephalomyelitis. *Neurocritical Care, 13,* 393–395.

Alderman, N. (2003). Contemporary approaches to the management of irritability and aggression following traumatic brain injury. *Neuropsychological Rehabilitation, 13,* 211–240.

American Congress of Rehabilitation Medicine. (1995). Locked-in syndrome. *Archives of Physical Medicine and Rehabilitation, 76,* 205–209.

Anderson, V. A., Dudgeon, P., Haritou, F., Catroppa, C., Morse, S. A., & Rosenfeld, J. V. (2006). Understanding predictors of functional recovery and outcome 30 months following early childhood head injury. *Neuropsychology, 20,* 42–57.

Andrews, K. (1997). Vegetative state – background and ethics. *Journal of the Royal Society of Medicine, 90,* 493–496.

Andrews, K., Murphy, L., Munday, R., & Littlewood, C. (1996). Misdiagnosis of the vegetative state: Retrospective study in a rehabilitation unit. *British Medical Journal, 313,* 13–16.

Andrews, K. (2005). Rehabilitation practice following profound brain damage. *Neuropsychological Rehabilitation, 15,* 461–472.

Angelino, E., Miglioretti, M., & Zotti, A. M. (2002). Agitation assessment in severe traumatic brain injury: Methodological and clinical issues. *Brain Injury, 16,* 269–275.

Ashford, L., Brooks, L., Cohen, P., Cummings, B., Griebel, M., Herman, L., . . . & Wittekind, P. (2013). *The peripatetic pursuit of Parkinson disease.* Little Rock, AR: The Parkinson's Creative Collective.

Aydin, S., Kucukyuruk, B., Abuzayed, B., Aydin, S., & Sanus, G. P. (2011). Cranioplasty: Review of materials and techniques. *Journal of Neurosciences in Rural Practice, 2,* 162–167.

Baguley, I., Cooper, J., & Felmingham, K. (2006). Aggressive behavior following traumatic brain injury: How common is common? *Journal of Head Trauma Rehabilitation, 21*, 45–56.

Barker, V. L., & Brunk, B. (1991). The role of a creative arts group in the treatment of clients with traumatic brain injury. *Music Therapy Perspectives, 9*, 26–31.

Bauby, J.-D. (1997). *The Diving Bell and the Butterfly (original title: La Scaphandre et le Papillon:* Robert Lafont: Paris). New York: Knopf.

Baussart, B., Cheisson, G., Compain, M., Leblanc, P. E., Tadie, M., Benhamou, D., et al. (2006). Multimodal cerebral monitoring and decompressive surgery for the treatment of severe bacterial meningitis with increased intracranial pressure. *Acta Anaesthesiologica Scandinavica, 50*, 762–765.

Baxter, A. G. (2007). The origin and application of experimental autoimmune encephalomyelitis. *Nature Reviews Immunology, 7*(11), 904–912.

Beaumont, J. G., Marjoribanks, J., Flury, S., & Lintern, T. (2002). *Putney auditory comprehension screening test* (PACST). London: Harcourt Assessment.

Beckinschtein, T., Tiberti, C., Niklison, J., Tamashiro, M., Ron, M., Carpintiero, S., . . . & Manes, F. (2005). Assessing level of consciousness and cognitive changes from vegetative state to full recovery. *Neuropsychological Rehabilitation, 15*, 307–322.

Bender, A., Heulin, S., Röhrer, S., Mehrkens, J. H., Heidecke, V., Straube, A., et al. (2013). Early cranioplasty may improve outcome in neurological patients with decompressive craniectomy. *Brain Injury, 27*(9), 1073–1079.

Bick, A. S., Mayer, A. M., & Levin, N. (2012). From research to clinical practice: Implementation of functional magnetic imaging and white matter tractography in the clinical environment. *Journal of the Neurological Sciences, 312*, 158–165.

Bigler, E. D. (2007). Traumatic brain injury and cognitive reserve. In Y. Stern (Ed.), *Cognitive reserve: Theory and applications* (pp. 85–116). New York: Taylor & Francis.

Bogner, J. A., Corrigan, J. D., Mysiw, W. J., Clinchot, D., & Fugate, L. (2001). A comparison of substance abuse and violence in the prediction of long-term rehabilitation outcomes after traumatic brain injury. *Archives of Physical Medicine and Rehabilitation, 82*(5), 571–577.

Boly, M., Faymonville, M. E., Peigneux, P., Lambermont, B., Damas, F., Luxen, A., . . . & Laureys, S. (2005). Cerebral processing of auditory and noxious stimuli in severely brain injured patients: Differences between VS and MCS. *Neuropsychological Rehabilitation, 15*, 283–289.

Borthwick, C. (2005). Ethics and the vegetative state. *Neuropsychological Rehabilitation, 15*(3–4), 257–263.

Büssing, A., Cysarz, D., Edelhäuser, F., Bornhöft, G., Matthiessen, P. F., & Ostermann, T. (2008). The oil-dispersion bath in anthroposophic medicine—an integrative review. *Complementary and Alternative Medicine, 8* doi:10.1186/1472–6882–8–61

Bütefisch, C. M. (2004). Plasticity in the human cerebral cortex: Lessons from the normal brain and from stroke. *The Neuroscientist, 10*(2), 163–173.

Cancelliere, C., Donovan, J., & Cassidy, J.D. (2015). Is sex an indicator of prognosis after mild traumatic brain injury: A systematic analysis of the findings of the WHO Collaborating Centre Task Force on Mild Traumatic Brain Injury and the International Collaboration on Mild Traumatic Brain Injury Prognosis. *Archives of Physical Medicine and Rehabilitation* 2015 Feb 6. pii: S0003–9993(15)00100–8. doi:10.1016/j.apmr.2014.11.028

Carlomagno, S., VanEeckhout, P., Blasi, V., Belin, P., Samson, Y., & Deloche, G. (1997). The impact of functional neuroimaging methods on the development of a theory for cognitive remediation. *Neuropsychological Rehabilitation, 7,* 311–326.

Cecatto, R. B., & Chadi, G. (2007). The importance of neuronal stimulation in central nervous system plasticity and neurorehabilitation strategies. *Functional Neurology, 22*(3), 137–143.

Chapman, L., Morabito, D., Ladakakos, C., Schreier, H., & Knudson, M. M. (2001). The effectiveness of art therapy interventions in reducing post traumatic stress disorder (PTSD) symptoms in pediatric trauma patients. *Journal of the American Art Therapy Association, 18,* 100–104.

Chieregato, A. (2006). The syndrome of the sunken skin flap: A neglected potentially reversible phenomenon affecting recovery after decompressive craniotomy. *Intensive Care Medicine, 32*(10), 1668–1669.

Childs, N. L., Mercer, W. N., & Childs, H. W. (1993). Accuracy of diagnosis of persistent vegetative state. *Neurology, 43,* 1465–1467.

Coleman, M. R., Rodd, J. M., Davis, M. H., Johnsrude, I. S., Menon, D. K., Pickard, J. D., & Owen, A. M. (2007). Do vegetative patients retain aspects of language comprehension? Evidence from fMRI. *Brain, 130,* 2494–507.

Coombes, K. (2008). Facial oral tract therapy (FOTT). *iADH Magazine*, Spring, 11–12.

Cruse, D., Chennu, S., Chatelle, C., Bekinschtein, T.A., Fernández-Espejo, D., Pickard, J., & Owen, A. M. (2012). Bedside detection of awareness in the vegetative state: A cohort study. *The Lancet, 378*(9809), 2088–2094.

Cushing, H. (1905). The establishment of cerebral hernia as a decompressive measure for inaccessible brain tumors; with the description of intramuscular methods of making the bone defect in temporal and occipital regions. *The Journal of Surgery, Gynaecology and Obstetrics, 1,* 297–314.

Daisley, A., Tams, R., & Kischka, U. (2009). *Head injury: The facts.* Oxford: Oxford University Press.

Davis, A. E. (2000). Cognitive impairments following traumatic brain injury. Etiologies and interventions. *Critical Care Nursing Clinics of North America, 12,* 447–456.

De Bonis, P., Frassanito, P., Mangiola, A., Nucci, C. G., Anile, C., & Pompucci, A. (2012). Cranial repair: How complicated is filling a "hole"? *Journal of Neurotrauma, 29,* 1071–1076.

Denmark, J., & Gemeinhardt, M. (2002). Anger and its management for survivors of acquired brain injury. *Brain Injury, 16*, 91–108.

Dewar, B.-K. (2014). Foreword. In B.A. Wilson, C. Robertson, & J. Mole, *Identity unknown: How acute brain disease can affect knowledge of oneself and others* (p. xiv). Hove, UK: Psychology Press.

Dewar, B.-K., Pickard, J.D., & Wilson, B.A. (2008). Long-term follow-up of 12 patients in the vegetative and minimally conscious states: An exploratory study. *Brain Impairment, 9*, 267–273.

Dhamapurkar, S., Wilson, B.A., Rose, A., & Florschutz, G. (2015, July). *Patterns of recovery from severe brain injury as measured by the Wessex Head Injury Matrix (WHIM)*. Poster presented at the 12th International Rehabilitation Congress, Daydream Island, Australia.

Di Stefano, C., Sturiale, C., Trentini, P., Bonora, R., Rossi, D., Cervigni, G., & Piperno, R. (2012). Unexpected neuropsychological improvement after cranioplasty: A case series study. *British Journal Neurosurgery, 26*(6), 827–831.

Douglas, P.E. (2014). *Thalamus.* Belgrade, MT: Christopher Matthews Publishing.

Duffau, H. (2006). Brain plasticity: From pathophysiological mechanisms to therapeutic applications. *Journal of Clinical Neuroscience, 13*(9), 885–897.

Elliott, L., Coleman, M., Shiel, A., Wilson, B.A., Badwan, D., Menon, D., & Pickard, J. (2005). Effect of posture on levels of arousal and awareness in vegetative and minimally conscious state patients: A preliminary investigation. *Journal of Neurology, Neurosurgery and Psychiatry, 76*, 298–299.

Elliott, L., & Walker, L. (2005). Rehabilitation interventions for vegetative and minimally conscious patients. *Neuropsychological Rehabilitation, 15*, 480–493.

Erdogan, E., Düz, B., Kocaoglu, M., Izci, Y., Sirin, S., & Timurkaynak, E. (2003). The effect of cranioplasty on cerebral hemodynamics: Evaluation with transcranial Doppler sonography. *Neurology India, 51*, 479–481.

Ernst, E. (2004). Anthroposophical medicine: A systematic review of randomised clinical trials. *Wien Klin Wochenschr, 116*, 128–130.

Farace, E., & Alves, W.M. (2000). Do women fare worse? A meta-analysis of gender differences in outcome after traumatic brain injury. *Neurosurgical Focus [electronic resource], 8*(1), e6.

Finger, S., Koehler, P.J., & Jagella, C. (2004). The Monakow concept of diaschisis: Origins and perspectives. *Archives of Neurology, 61*(2), 283–288.

Flint, A.C., Manley, G.T., Gean, A.D., Hemphill, J.C. III, & Rosenthal, G. (2008). Post-operative expansion of hemorrhagic contusions after unilateral decompressive hemicraniectomy in severe traumatic brain injury. *Journal of Neurotrauma, 25*(5), 503–512.

Fodstad, H., Love, J.A., Ekstedt, J., Fridén, H., & Liliequist, B. (1984). Effect of cranioplasty on cerebrospinal fluid hydrodynamics in patients with the syndrome of the trephined. *Acta Neurochirurgica, 70*(1–2), 21–30.

Forsyth, R. J., Wong C. P., Kelly, T. P., Borrill, H., Stilgoe, D., Kendall, S., & Eyre, J. A. (2001). Cognitive and adaptive outcomes and age at insult effects after non-traumatic coma. *Archives of Disease in Childhood, 84,* 200–204.

Foster, R. D., Antonyshyn, O. M., Lee, C., Holland, M., & Fazl, M. (2002). Cranioplasty: Indications, techniques, and results. In H. H. Schmidek (Ed.), *Schmidek and Sweet: Operative neurosurgical techniques* (pp. 29–44). Philadelphia: WB Saunders.

Friedland, D., & Hutchinson, P. (2013). Classification of traumatic brain injury. *Advances in Clinical Neuroscience & Rehabilitation, 4,* 12–13.

Giacino, J. T., Ashwal, S., Childs, N., Cranford, R., Jennett, B., Katz, D. I., . . . & Zasler, N. D. (2002). The minimally conscious state: Definition and diagnostic criteria. *Neurology, 2002,* 58, 349–353.

Giacino, J. T., Hirsch, J., Schiff, N., & Laureys, S. (2006). Functional neuroimaging applications for assessment and rehabilitation planning in patients with disorders of consciousness. *Archives of Physical Medicine and Rehabilitation, 2006, 87*(12 Suppl 2), S67–76.

Giacino, J. T., & Kalmar, K. (1997). The vegetative and minimally conscious states: A comparison of clinical features and functional outcome. *Journal of Head Trauma Rehabilitation, 12*(4), 36–51.

Giacino, J. T., & Kalmar, K. (2005). Diagnostic and prognostic guidelines for the vegetative and minimally conscious states. *Neuropsychological Rehabilitation, 15,* 166–174.

Giacino, J., Kalmar, K., & Whyte, J. (2004). The JFK Coma Recovery Scale-Revised: Measurement characteristics and diagnostic utility. *Archives of Physical Medicine and Rehabilitation, 85,* 2020–2029.

Giacino, J., & Whyte, J. (2005). The vegetative and minimally conscious states: Current knowledge and remaining questions. *Journal of Head Trauma Rehabilitation, 20,* 30–50.

Golding, E. (1989). *The Middlesex elderly assessment of mental state.* Bury St Edmunds: Thames Valley Test Company.

Gordon, W. A., Zafonte, R., Cicerone, K., Cantor, J., Brown, M., Lombard, L., . . . & Chandna, T. (2006). Traumatic brain injury rehabilitation: State of science. *American Journal of Physical Medicine & Rehabilitation, 85,* 343–82.

Granger, C. V., Hamilton, B. B., Keith, R. A., Zielezny, M., & Sherwin, F. S. (1986). Advances in functional assessment for medical rehabilitation. *Topics in Geriatric Rehabilitation, 1,* 59–74.

Guérit, J. M. (2005). Evoked potentials in severe brain injury. *Progress in Brain Research, 150,* 415–426.

Güresir, E., Schuss, P., Vatter, H., Raabe, A., Seifert, V., & Beck, J. (2009). Decompressive craniectomy in subarachnoid hemorrhage. *Neurosurgical Focus, 26,* E4.

Hall, G. R., & Buckwalter, K. C. (1987). Progressively lowered stress threshold: A conceptual model for care of adults with Alzheimer's disease. *Achieves Psychiatric Nursing, 1*(6), 399–406.

Hall, K.M., Hamilton, B.B., Gordon, W.A., & Zasler, N.D. (1993). Characteristics and comparisons of functional assessment indices: Disability Rating Scale, Functional Independence Measure and Functional Assessment Measure. *Journal of Head Trauma Rehabilitation, 8,* 60–74.

Hessen, E., Nestvold, K., & Anderson, V.A. (2007). Neuropsychological function 23 years after mild traumatic brain injury: A comparison of outcome after paediatric and adult head injuries. *Brain Injury, 21,* 963–979.

Honeybul, S., Janzen, C., Kruger, K., & Ho, K.M. (2013). The impact of cranioplasty on neurological function. *British Journal of Neurosurgery, 27*(5), 636–641.

Humphreys, G.W., & Riddoch, M.J. (1987). *To see but not to see: A case study of visual agnosia.* Hillsdale, NJ: Lawrence Erlbaum Associates.

Humphreys, G.W., & Riddoch, M.J. (2013). *A case study in visual agnosia revisited: To see but not to see* (2nd ed.). Hove, UK: Psychology Press.

Isago, T., Nozaki, M., Kikuchi, Y., Honda, T., & Nakazawa, H. (2004). Sinking skin flap syndrome: A case of improved cerebral blood flow after cranioplasty. *Annals of Plastic Surgery, 53,* 288–292.

James, A.B. (2003). Theories derived from rehabilitation perspectives. Biomechanical frame of reference. In E.B. Crepeau, E.S. Cohn, & B.A.B. Schell (Eds.), *Willard and Speckman's occupational therapy* (10th ed., pp. 235–242). Philadelphia, PA: Lippincott, Williams and Wilkins.

Jang, S.H., You, S.H., & Ahn, S.H. (2007). Neurorehabilitation-induced cortical reorganization in brain injury: A 14-month longitudinal follow-up study. *NeuroRehabilitation, 22,* 117–122.

Jelcic, N., De Pellegrin, S., Cecchin, D., Della Puppa, A., & Cagnin, A. (2013). Cognitive improvement after cranioplasty: A possible volume transmission-related effect. *Acta Neurochirurgica, 155,* 1597–1599.

Jennett, B. (1990). Scale and scope of the problems. In M. Rosenthal, E.R. Griffith, M.R. Bond, & J.D. Miller (Eds.), *Rehabilitation of the adult and child with traumatic brain injury* (pp. 3–7). Philadelphia: F.A. Davis and Co.

Jennett, B. (2005). Foreword to Coleman, M. (ed.), The assessment and rehabilitation of vegetative and minimally conscious patients. *Neuropsychological Rehabilitation (Special Issue), 15,* 163.

Jennett, B., & Bond, M. (1975). Assessment of outcome after severe brain damage. *Lancet, 1*(7905), 480–484.

Jennett, B., & Plum, F. (1972). Persistent vegetative state after brain damage. A syndrome in search of a name. *Lancet, 1*(7753), 734–737.

Johansson, B.B. (2007). Regeneration and plasticity in the brain and spinal cord. *Journal of Cerebral Blood Flow and Metabolism, 27,* 1417–1430.

Johnson, D.A., Rose, F.D., Brooks, B.M., & Eyers, S. (2003). Age and recovery from brain injury: Legal opinions, clinical beliefs and experimental evidence. *Pediatric Rehabilitation, 6*(2), 103–109.

Johnson, V.E., & Stewart, W. (2014). Traumatic brain injury: Age at injury influences dementia risk after TBI. *Nature Reviews Neurology.* doi:10.1038/nrneurol.2014.241 Published online 23 December 2014.

Joseph, V., & Reilly, P. (2009). Syndrome of the trephined. *Journal of Neurosurgery, 111*, 650–652.

Kakar V., Nagaria, J., & Kirkpatick, P. (2009). The current status of decompressive craniectomy. *British Journal of Neurosurgery, 23*, 147–157.

Kalmar, K., & Giacino, J.T. (2005). The JFK Coma Recovery Scale-Revised. *Neuropsychological Rehabilitation, 15*, 454–460.

Kaplan, S., & Kaplan, R. (1982). *Cognitive and environment: Functioning in an uncertain world.* New York: Praeger.

Kemmling, A., Duning, T., Lemcke, L., et al. (2010). Case report of MR perfusion imaging in sinking skin flap syndrome: Growing evidence for hemodynamic impairment. *BMC Neurology, 10*, 80.

Kienle, G.S., Kienle, H., & Albonico, H.U. (2006). Anthroposophic medicine: Health technology assessment report. *Forsch Komplementmed, 13*(suppl 2), 7–18.

Kolb, B. (1995). *Brain plasticity and behaviour.* Hillsdale, NJ: Lawrence Erlbaum.

Konczak, J., Schoch, B., Dimitrova, A., Gizewski, E., & Timmann, D. (2005). Functional recovery of children and adolescents after cerebellar tumour resection. *Brain, 128*, 1428–1441.

Kotchoubey, B. (2005). Appallic syndrome is not appallic: Is vegetative state vegetative? *Neuropsychological Rehabilitation, 15*, 333–356.

Kretschmer, E. (1940). Das apallische Syndrome. *Zeitschrift fur gesante Neurologie ind Psychiatrie, 169*, 576–579.

Kumar, G.S., Chacko, A.G., & Rajshekhar, V. (2004). Unusual presentation of the "syndrome of the trephined." *Neurology India, 52*, 504–505.

Kuo, J.R., Wang, C.C., Chio, C.C., & Cheng, T.J. (2004). Neurological improvement after cranioplasty-analysis by transcranial Doppler ultrasonography. *Journal of Clinical Neuroscience, 11*, 486–489.

Laatsch, L., Pavel, D., Jobe, T., Lin, Q., & Quintana, J.C. (1999). Incorporation of SPECT imaging in a longitudinal cognitive rehabilitation therapy programme. *Brain Injury, 13*, 555–570.

Laatsch, L., Thomas, J., Sychra, J., Qing, L., & Blend, M. (1997). Impact of cognitive rehabilitation therapy on neuropsychological impairments as measured by brain perfusion SPECT: A longitudinal study. *Brain Injury, 11*, 851–864.

Laatsch, L.K., Thulborn, K.R., Krisky, C.M., Shobat, D.M., & Sweeney, J.A. (2004). Investigating the neurobiological basis of cognitive rehabilitation therapy with fMRI. *Brain Injury, 18*, 957–974.

Laureys, S., Celesi, G.G., Cohadon, F., Lavrijsen, J., León-Carrión, J., Sannita, W.G., ... & the European Task Force on Disorders of Consciousness. (2010). Unresponsive wakefulness syndrome: A new name for the vegetative state or apallic syndrome. *BMC Medicine, 8.* doi:10.1186/1741-7015-8-68

Laureys, S., Pellas, F., Van Eeckhout, P., Ghorbel, S., Schnakers, C., Perrin, F., ... & Goldman, S. (2005). The locked-in syndrome: What is it like to be conscious but paralyzed and voiceless? *Progress in Brain Research, 150*, 495–511.

Lenzlinger, P. M., Morganti-Kossmann, M. C., Laurer, H. L., & McIntosh, T. K. (2001). The duality of the inflammatory response to traumatic brain injury. *Molecular Neurobiology, 24,* 169–181.

Levin, H. S. (2003). Neuroplasticity following non-penetrating traumatic brain injury. *Brain Injury, 17* 667–674.

Lindgren, M., Österberg, K., Ørbæk, P., & Rosén, I. (1997). Solvent-induced toxic encephalopathy: Electrophysiological data in relation to neuropsychological findings. *Journal of Clinical and Experimental Neuropsychology, 19,* 772–783.

Lippe, S., Gonin-Flambois, C., & Jambaqué, I. (2012). The neuropsychology of the Kluver-Bucy syndrome in children. *Handbook of Clinical Neurology, 112,* 1285–1288.

Logan, A., Oliver, J. J., & Berry, M. (2007). Growth factors in CNS repair and regeneration. *Progress in Growth Factor Research,* 379–406.

Luauté, J., Maucort-Boulch, D., Tell, L., Quelard, F., Sarraf, T., Iwaz, J., . . . & Fischer, C. (2010). Long-term outcomes of chronic minimally conscious and vegetative states. *Neurology, 75,* 246–252.

Luria, A. R., & Solotaroff, L. (1987). *The man with a shattered world: The history of a brain wound.* Boston, MA: Harvard University Press.

Ma, Zhang, Li Ma, J., Zhang C.-G., & Li, Y. (2007). Bone marrow stromal cells transplantation for traumatic brain injury. *Journal of Clinical Rehabilitative Tissue Engineering Research, 11,* 2932–2935.

Macmillan, M. (2000). *An odd kind of fame: Stories of Phineas Gage.* Cambridge: MIT Press.

Maeshima, S., Kagawa, M., Kishida, Y., Kobayashi, K., Makabe, T., Morita, Y., . . . & Tsubahara, A. (2005). Unilateral spatial neglect related to a depressed skin flap following decompressive craniectomy. *European Neurology, 53,* 164–168.

Magee, W. L. (2005). Music therapy with patients in low awareness states: Approaches to assessment and treatment in multidisciplinary care. *Neuropsychological Rehabilitation, 15,* 522–536.

Marjerus, S., Van Der Linden, M., & Shiel, A. (2000). The Wessex Head Injury Matrix and the Glasgow/Glasgow-Liege coma scale: A validation and comparison study. *Neuropsychological Rehabilitation, 10,* 167–184.

Marshall, J. F. (1985). Neural plasticity and recovery of function after brain injury. *International Review of Neurobiology, 26,* 201–447.

McLellan, D. L. (1991). Functional recovery and the principles of disability medicine. In M. Swash & J. Oxbury (Eds.), *Clinical neurology* (pp. 768–790). Edinburgh: Churchill Livingstone.

Menon, D. K., Owen, A. M., Williams, E. J., Minhas, P. S., Allen, C.M.C., Boniface, S. J., & Pickard, J. D. (1998). Cortical processing in persistent vegetative state. *Lancet, 352*(9123), 200.

Menon, D. K., Schwab, K., Wright, D. W., & Maas, A. I. (2010). On behalf of the Demographics and Clinical Assessment Working Group of the International and Interagency Initiative toward Common Data Elements for Research on Traumatic Brain Injury and Psychological Health. *Archives of Physical Medicine and Rehabilitation, 91*, 1637–1640. doi:10.1016/j.apmr.2010.05.017

Miller, E. (1984). *Recovery and management of neuropsychological function*. Chichester, UK: Wiley.

Miller, J. D., Pentland, B., & Berrol, S. (1990). Early evaluation and management. In M. Rosenthal, E. R. Griffith, M. R. Bond, & J. D. Miller (Eds.), *Rehabilitation of the adult and child with traumatic brain injury* (pp. 21–51). Philadelphia: Davis.

Millis, S. R., Rosenthal, M., Novack, T. A., Sherer, M., Nick, T. G., Kreutzer, J. S., . . . & Ricker, J. H. (2001). Long-term neuropsychological outcome after traumatic brain injury. *The Journal of Head Trauma Rehabilitation, 16*(4), 343–355.

Montour-Proulx, I., Braun, C.M.J., Daigneault, S., Rouleau, I., Kuehn, S., & Oégin, J. (2004). Predictors of intellectual function after a unilateral cortical lesion: Study of 635 patients from infancy to adulthood. *Journal of Child Neurology, 19*, 935–943.

Mosch, S. C., Max, J. E., & Tranel, D. (2005). A matched lesion analysis of childhood versus adult-onset brain injury due to unilateral stroke: Another perspective on neural plasticity and recovery of social functioning. *Cognitive & Behavioral Neurology, 18*, 5–17.

The Multi-Society Task Force. (1994). Report on PVS. Medical aspects of the persistent vegetative state. *New England Journal of Medicine, 330*, 1499–1508, 1572–1579.

Nudo, R. J. (2013). Recovery after brain injury: Mechanisms and principles. *Frontiers in Human Neuroscience, 7*, 887.

Nunnari, D., Bramanti, P., & Marino, S. (2014). Cognitive reserve in stroke and traumatic brain injury patients. *Neurological Sciences 2014 October, 35*(10), 1513–1518. doi:10.1007/s10072–014–1897-z. Epub 2014 Jul 23.

Owen, A., & Coleman, M. (2008). Detecting awareness in the vegetative state. *Annals of the New York Academy of Science 1129*, 130–138. doi:10.1196/annals.1417.018

Owen, A. M., Coleman, M. R., Boly, M., Davis, M. H., Laureys, S., & Pickard, J. D. (2007). Using functional magnetic resonance imaging to detect covert awareness in the vegetative state. *Archives of Neurology, 64*, 1098–1102.

Padovan, B.A.E. (1992). *Neurologische Reorganization und ihr Nutzen für behinderte Kinder. Heilpädagogischer Kongress – Lebensqualität und Heilpädagogik.* Innsbruck, Verlag Kaiser.

Parr, A. M., Tator, C. H., & Keating, A. (2007). Bone marrow-derived mesenchymal stromal cells for the repair of central nervous system injury. *Bone Marrow Transplantation, 40*, 609–619.

Pickard, J. D., Coleman, M. R., & Czosnyka, M. (2005). Hydrocephalus, ventriculomegaly and the vegetative state: A review. *Neuropsychological Rehabilitation, 15*, 224–236.

Pizzamiglio, L., Perani, D., Cappa, S. F., Vallar, G., Paolucci, S., Grassi, F., . . . & Fazio, F. (1998). Recovery of neglect after right hemispheric damage: H215O positron emission tomographic activation study. *Archives of Neurology, 55*(4), 561–568.

Ponsford, J. L., Myles, P. S., Cooper, D. J., McDermott, F. T., Murray, L. J., Laidlaw, J., & Cooper, G. (2008). Gender differences in outcome in patients with hypotension and severe traumatic brain injury. *Injury, 39,* 67–76.

Province, C. (2005). The vegetative state: Promoting greater clarity and improved treatment. *Neuropsychological Rehabilitation, 15,* 264–271.

Rappoport, M. (2005). The Disability Rating and Coma/Near Coma scales in evaluating severe head injury. *Neuropsychological Rehabilitation, 15,* 442–453.

Ratcliff, J. J., Greenspan, A. I., Goldstein, F. C., Stringer, A. Y., Bushnik, T., Hammond, F. M., . . . & Wright, D. W. (2007). Gender and traumatic brain injury: Do the sexes fare differently? *Brain Injury, 21,* 1023–1030.

Reimer, M., & LeNavenec C.-L. (2005). Rehabilitation and outcome evaluation after very severe brain injury. *Neuropsychological Rehabilitation, 15,* 473–479.

Rish, B. L., Dillon, J. D., Meirowsky, A. M., Caveness, W. F., Mohr, J. P., Kistler, J. P., & et al. (1979). Cranioplasty: A review of 1030 cases of penetrating head injury. *Neurosurgery, 4,* 381–385.

Roberts, C. B., Rafal, R., & Coetzer, B. R. (2006). Feedback of brain-imaging findings: Effect on impaired awareness and mood in acquired brain injury. *Brain Injury, 20*(5), 485–497.

Roberts, M. (2005). A brief overview of occupational therapy theories, models and frames of reference. In A. Wagenfeld & J. Kaldenberg (Eds.), *Foundations of pediatric practice* (pp. 17–22). Thorofare, NJ: Slack.

Robertson, I. H. (2002). Cognitive neuroscience and brain rehabilitation: a promise kept. *Journal of Neurology, Neurosurgery & Psychiatry, 73,* 357–357.

Robertson, I. H., & Murre, J.M.J. (1999). Rehabilitation after brain damage: Brain plasticity and principles of guided recovery. *Psychological Bulletin, 125,* 544–575.

Roof, R. L., & Hall, E. D. (2000). Gender differences in acute CNS trauma and stroke: Neuroprotective effects of estrogen and progesterone. *Journal of Neurotrauma, 17,* 367–388.

Rosenblum, W. I. (2015). Immediate, irreversible, post-traumatic coma: A review indicating that bilateral brainstem injury rather than widespread hemispheric damage is essential for its production. *Journal of Neuropathology and Experimenental Neurology, 74,* 198–202.

Royal College of Physicians. (2003). *The vegetative state: Guidance on diagnosis and management.* London: Author.

Royal College of Physicians. (2013). *Prolonged disorders of consciousness: National clinical guidelines.* London: Author.

Rusk, H. A., Loman, E. W., & Block, L. M. (1966). Rehabilitation of the patient with head injury. *Clinical Neurosurgery, 12,* 312–323.

Schneider, E. B., Sur, S., Raymont, V., Duckworth, J., Kowalski, R. G., Efron, D. T., & Stevens, R. D. (2014). Functional recovery after moderate/severe traumatic brain injury. A role for cognitive reserve? *Neurology, 82,* 1636–1642.

Scholz, J., Klein, M. C., Behrens, T.E.J., & Johansen-Berg, H. (2009). Training induces changes in white-matter architecture. *Nature Neuroscience, 12,* 1370–1371.

Schuss, P., Vatter, H., Marquardt, G., Imöhl, L., Ulrich, C. T., Seifert, V., et al. (2012). Cranioplasty after decompressive craniectomy: The effect of timing on postoperative complications. *Journal of Neurotrauma, 29,* 1090–1095.

Schutz, L. E. (2007). Models of exceptional adaptation in recovery after traumatic brain injury: A case series. *Journal of Head Trauma Rehabilitation, 22,* 48–55.

Sharma, A., Sane, H., Kulkarni, P., Yadav, J., Gokulchandran, N., Biju, H., & Badhe, P. (2015). Cell therapy attempted as a novel approach for chronic traumatic brain injury–a pilot study. *SpringerPlus, 4,* 26.

Shiel, A. (1999). *Assessment and recovery of cognitive behaviours and cognitive impairment after severe traumatic brain injury.* Unpublished PhD thesis. University of Southampton.

Shiel, A., Wilson, B. A., McLellan, L., Horn, S., & Watson, M. (2000). *The Wessex Head Injury Matrix (WHIM).* Bury St Edmunds: Thames Valley Test Company.

Skolnick, B. E., Maas, A. I., Narayan, R. K., van der Hoop, R. G., MacAllister, T., Ward, J. D., . . . & Stocchetti, N. (2014). A clinical trial of progesterone for severe traumatic brain injury. *New England Journal of Medicine, 37,* 2467–2476.

Sorbo, A., Rydenhag, B., Sunnerhagen, K. S., Blomqvist, M., Svensson, S., & Emanuelson, I. (2004). Outcome after severe brain damage, what makes a difference? *Brain Injury, 19,* 493–503.

Stein, D. G. (2007). Brain damage, sex hormones and recovery: A new role for progesterone and estrogen? *Trends in Neurosciences, 24,* 386–391.

Stein, D. G., & Hoffman, S. W. (2003). Concepts of CNS plasticity in the context of brain damage and repair. *Journal of Head Trauma Rehabilitation, 18,* 317–341.

Stern, Y. (2007). *Cognitive reserve: Theory and applications.* New York: Taylor & Francis.

Stinear, C. M., & Ward, N. S. (2013). How useful is imaging in predicting outcomes in stroke rehabilitation? *International Journal of Stroke, 8,* 33–37.

Stiver, S. I., Wintermark, M., & Manley, G. T. (2008). Motor trephine syndrome: A mechanistic hypothesis. *Acta Neurochirurgica Supplement, 102,* 273–277.

Stuss, D. T., Binns, M. A., Carruth, F. G., Levine, B., Brandys, C. E., Moulton, R. J., . . . & Schwartz, M. L. (1999). The acute period of recovery from traumatic brain injury: Posttraumatic amnesia or posttraumatic confusional state? *Journal of Neurosurgery, 90,* 635–643.

Sulaiman, S. (2007). *Learning to live with Huntington's Disease: One family's story.* London: Jessica Kingsley Publishers.

Symonds, C. P. (1937). Mental disorder following head injury. *Proceedings of the Royal Society of Medicine, 30,* 1081–1092.

Tasiou, A., Vagkopoulos, K., Georgiadis, I., Brotis, A. G., Gatos, H., & Fountas, K. N. (2014). Cranioplasty optimal timing in cases of decompressive craniectomy after severe head injury: A systematic literature review. *Interdisciplinary Neurosurgery, 1*(4), 107–111.

Taupin, P. (2006). Adult neurogenesis and neuroplasticity. *Restorative Neurology and Neuroscience, 24,* 9–15.

Tavano, A., Galbiati, S., Recla, M., Bardoni, A., Dominici, C., Pastore, V., & Strazzer, S. (2014). Cognitive recovery after severe traumatic brain injury in children/adolescents and adults: Similar positive outcome but different underlying pathways? *Brain Injury, 28*(7), 900–905.

Thaut, M., & McIntosh, G. (2010, March). How music helps to heal the injured brain; therapeutic use crescendos thanks to advances in brain science. *Cerebrum,* 1–12.

Thavarajah, D., De Lacy, P., Hussien, A., & Sugar, A. (2012). The minimum time for cranioplasty insertion from craniectomy is six months to reduce risk of infection—a case series of 82 patients. *British Journal of Neurosurgery, 26,* 78–80.

Upledger, J. E., & Karni, Z. (1979). Mechano-electric patterns during craniosacral osteopathic diagnosis and treatment. *The Journal of the American Osteopathic Association, 78,* 782–791.

van der Werf, M. J., de Vlas, S. J., Brooker, S., Looman, C. W., Nagelkerke, N. J., Habbema, J.D.F., & Engels, D. (2003). Quantification of clinical morbidity associated with schistosome infection in sub-Saharan Africa. *Acta Tropica, 86*(2), 125–139.

Voelbel, G. T., Genova, H. M., Chiaravalotti, N. D., & Hoptman, M. J. (2012). Diffusion tensor imaging of traumatic brain injury review: Implications for neurorehabilitation. *NeuroRehabilitation, 31,* 281–293. doi:10.3233/NRE-2012–0796

Von Monakow, C. (1914). *Die Lokalisation im Grosshirn und der Abbau der Funktion durch kortikale Herde.* Wiesbaden, Germany: JF Bergmann.

Voss, H. U., Ulŭg, A. M., Dyke, J. P., Watts, R., Kobylarz, E. J., McCandliss, B. D., . . . & Schiff, N. D. (2006). Possible axonal regrowth in late recovery from the minimally conscious state. *Journal of Clinical Investigation, 116,* 2005–2011.

Warrington, E. K., & James, M. (1991). *The visual object and space perception battery.* Bury St Edmunds: Thames Valley Test Company.

Warrington, E. K., Plant, J., & James, M. (2001). *The cortical vision screening Test.* Bury St Edmunds: Thames Valley Test Company.

Wearing, D. (2005). *Forever today: A memoir of love and amnesia.* London: Doubleday.

Wechsler, D. (2008). *The Wechsler adult intelligence scale – fourth edition (WAIS-IV).* San Antonio, TX: NCS Pearson.

Whyte, J. (1990). Mechanisms of recovery of function following CNS damage. In M. Rosenthal, E. R. Griffith, M. R. Bond, & J. D. Miller (Eds.), *Rehabilitation of the adult and child with TBI* (2nd ed., pp. 79–87). Philadelphia: F. A. Davis and Co.

Wilde, E. A., Hunter, J. V., & Bigler, E. D. (2012). A primer of neuroimaging analysis in neurorehabilitation outcomes research. *Neurorehabilitation, 31,* 227–243.

Wilson, B. A. (1982). Success and failure in memory training following a cerebral vascular accident. *Cortex, 18,* 581–594.

Wilson, B. A. (1999). *Case studies in neuropsychological rehabilitation.* New York: Oxford University Press.

Wilson, B. A. (2010). Brain damage & recovery. In L. Nadel & M. Corballis (Eds.), *Wiley interdisciplinary reviews: Cognitive neuroscience* [online]. Chichester, UK: Wiley & Son.

Wilson, B. A., Baddeley, A. D., & Kapur, N. (1995). Dense amnesia in a professional musician following herpes simplex virus encephalitis. *Journal of Clinical and Experimental Psychology, 17,* 668–681.

Wilson, B. A., & Bainbridge, K. (2014). Kate's Story: Recovery takes time, so don't give up. In B. A. Wilson, J. Winegardner, & F. Ashworth, *Life After Brain Injury: Survivors Stories* (pp. 50–62). Hove, UK: Psychology Press.

Wilson, B. A., Dhamapurkar, S., Tunnard, C., Watson, P., & Florschutz, G. (2013). The effect of positioning on the level of arousal and awareness in patients in the vegetative state or the minimally conscious state: A replication and extension of a previous finding. *Brain Impairment, 14,* 475–479.

Wilson, B. A., Gracey, F., & Bainbridge, K. (2001). Cognitive recovery from "persistent vegetative state": Psychological and personal perspectives. *Brain Injury, 15,* 1083–1092.

Wilson, B. A., Kopelman, M., & Kapur, N. (2008). Prominent and persistent loss of self-awareness in amnesia: delusion, impaired consciousness or coping strategy? *Neuropsychological Rehabilitation, 18,* 527–540.

Wilson, B. A., Robertson, C., & Mole, J. (2015). *Identity unknown: How acute brain disease can affect knowledge of oneself and others.* Hove, UK: Psychology Press.

Wilson, B. A., Rous, R., & Sopena, S. (2008). The current practice of neuropsychological rehabilitation in the United Kingdom. *Applied Neuropsychology, 15,* 229–240.

Wilson, B. A., & Okines, T. (2014). Tracey's story: Quality of life with locked-in syndrome. In B. A. Wilson, J. Winegardner, & F. Ashworth (Eds.), *Life After Brain Injury: Survivors Stories* (pp. 75–83). Hove, UK: Psychology Press.

Wilson, C., Graham, L. E., & Watson, T. (2005). Vegetative and minimally conscious states: Serial assessment approaches in diagnosis and management. *Neuropsychological Rehabilitation, 15,* 431–444.

Worsely, M. (2009). The jousting accident that turned Henry VIII into a tyrant. *The Independent* Newspaper (18 April 2009).

Wright, D. W., Kellermann, A. L., Hertzberg, V. S., Clark, P. L., Frankel, M., Goldstein, F. C., . . . & Stein, D. G. (2007). ProTECT: A randomized clinical trial of progesterone for acute traumatic brain injury. *Annals of Emergency Medicine, 49*, 391–402.

Yang, X. J., Hong, G. L., Su, S. B., & Yang, S. Y. (2003). Complications induced by decompressive craniectomies after traumatic brain injury. *Chinese Journal of Traumatology, 6*, 99–103.

Index